INTERACTIVE WHITEBOARD ACTIVITIES

Grades 4–6

Reading & Writing LESSONS FOR THE SMART BOARD™

Motivating, Interactive Lessons That Teach Key Reading & Writing Skills

SCHOLASTIC

New York ◦ Toronto ◦ London ◦ Auckland ◦ Sydney
New Delhi ◦ Mexico City ◦ Hong Kong ◦ Buenos Aires

Author: Eileen Jones
Illustrators: Jim Peacock (book and Notebook file illustrations), William Gray, Theresa Tibbetts (additional Notebook file illustrations), Andy Keylock (book illustrations), Garry Davies (Notebook files and book illustrations)
Editor: Maria L. Chang
Cover design: Brian LaRossa
Interior design: Grafica Inc.

CD-ROM developed in association with Q & D Multimedia

Special thanks to Robin Hunt and Melissa Rugless of Scholastic Ltd.

All Flash activities designed and developed by Q & D Multimedia.

ISBN: 978-0-545-29040-1

Printed in the U.S.A.

2 3 4 5 6 7 8 9 10 40 18 17 16 15 14 13 12 11

Contents

Introduction

Interactive whiteboards are fast becoming the must-have resource in today's classroom as they allow teachers to facilitate children's learning in ways that were inconceivable a few years ago. The appropriate use of interactive whiteboards, whether used daily in the classroom or once a week in a computer lab, encourages active participation in lessons and increases students' determination to succeed. Interactive whiteboards make it easier for teachers to bring subjects across the curriculum to life in new and exciting ways.

What can an interactive whiteboard offer?

For teachers, an interactive whiteboard allows them to do the same things they can on an ordinary whiteboard, such as drawing, writing, and erasing. However, the interactive whiteboard also offers many other possibilities, such as:

- saving any work created during a lesson;
- preparing as many pages as necessary;
- displaying any page within the Notebook™ file to review teaching and learning;
- adding scanned examples of the children's work to a Notebook file;
- changing colors of shapes and backgrounds instantly;
- using simple templates and grids;
- linking Notebook files to spreadsheets, Web sites, and presentations.

Using an interactive whiteboard in the simple ways outlined above can enrich teaching and learning in a classroom, but that is only the beginning of the whiteboard's potential to educate and inspire.

For students, the interactive whiteboard provides the opportunity to share learning experiences, as lessons can be delivered with sound, still and moving images, and Web sites. Interactive whiteboards can be used to cater to the needs of all learning styles:

- Kinesthetic learners benefit from being able to physically manipulate images.
- Visual learners benefit from being able to watch videos, look at photographs, and see images being manipulated.
- Auditory learners benefit from being able to access audio resources, such as voice recordings and sound effects.

With a little preparation, all of these resource types could be integrated into one lesson—a feat that would have been almost impossible before the advent of the interactive whiteboard!

Access to an interactive whiteboard

In schools where students have limited access to an interactive whiteboard, carefully planned lessons will help students get the most benefit from it during the times they can use it. As teachers become familiar with the interactive whiteboard, they will learn when to use it and, equally important, when not to use it!

Where permanent access to an interactive whiteboard is available, it is important to plan the use of the board effectively. It should be used only in ways that will enhance or extend teaching and learning. Children still need to gain practical, first-hand experience of many things. Some experiences cannot be recreated on an interactive whiteboard, but others cannot be had without it. *Reading & Writing Lessons for the SMART Board™* offers both teachers and learners the most accessible and creative uses of this most valuable resource.

About the book

Adapted from Scholastic UK's best-selling 100 SMART Board™ Lessons series, *Reading & Writing Lessons for the SMART Board™* is designed to reflect best practice in using interactive whiteboards. It is also designed to support all teachers in using this valuable tool by providing lessons and other resources that can be used on the SMART Board with little or no preparation. These inspirational lessons meet the English language arts Common Core State Standards and are perfect for all levels of experience.

This book is divided into four chapters. Each chapter contains lessons covering:

- Spelling & Vocabulary
- Writing
- Reading
- Grammar, Mechanics & Usage

Mini-Lessons

The mini-lessons have a consistent structure that includes:

- a **Getting Started** activity;
- a step-by-step **Mini-Lesson** plan;
- an **Independent Work** activity; and
- a **Wrap-Up** activity to round up the teaching and learning and identify any assessment opportunities.

Each mini-lesson identifies any resources required (including Notebook files that are provided on the CD-ROM, as well as reproducible activity pages) and lists the whiteboard tools that could be used in the mini-lesson.

The reproducible activity sheets toward the back of the book support the mini-lessons. These sheets provide opportunities for group or individual work to be completed away from the board, while linking to the context of the whiteboard lesson. They also provide opportunities for whole-class discussions in which children present their work.

What's on the CD-ROM?

The accompanying CD-ROM provides an extensive bank of Notebook files designed for use with the SMART Board. These support, and are supported by, the mini-lessons in this book. They can be annotated and saved for reference or for use with subsequent lessons; they can also be printed out. In addition to texts and images, a selection of Notebook files include the following types of files:

- **Embedded Microsoft Word files:** The embedded files are launched from the Notebook file and will open in their native Microsoft application.
- **Embedded interactive files:** These include specially commissioned interactive files that will open in a new browser window within the Notebook environment.
- **Embedded audio files:** Some Notebook files contain buttons that play sounds.
- **"Build Your Own" file:** This contains a blank Notebook page with a bank of selected images and interactive tools from the Gallery, as well as specially commissioned images. You can use this to help build your own Notebook files.

The Notebook files

All of the Notebook files have a consistent structure as follows:

- **Title and objectives page**—Use this page to highlight the focus of the mini-lesson. You might also wish to refer to this page at certain times throughout the lesson or at the end of the lesson to assess whether the learning objective was achieved.
- **Getting Started activity**—This sets the context to the lesson and usually provides some key questions or learning points that will be addressed through the main activities.
- **Main activities**—These activities offer independent, collaborative group, or whole-class work. The activities draw on the full scope of Notebook software and the associated tools, as well as the SMART Board tools. "What to Do" boxes are also included in many of the prepared Notebook files. These appear as tabs in the top right-hand corner of the screen. To access these notes, simply pull out the tabs to reveal planning information, additional support, and key learning points.
- **Wrap-Up**—A whole-class activity or summary page is designed to review work done both at the board and away from the board. In many lessons, children are encouraged to present their work.

How to Use the CD-ROM

Setting up your screen for optimal use

It is best to view the Notebook pages at a screen display setting of 1280 x 1024 pixels. To alter the screen display, select Settings, then Control Panel from the Start menu. Next, double-click on the Display icon, then click on the Settings tab. Finally, adjust the Screen area scroll bar to 1280 x 1024 pixels. Click on OK. (On the Mac, click on the apple icon and select System Preferences. Then click on Displays and select 1280 x 1024.)

If you prefer to use a screen display setting of 800 x 600 pixels, ensure that your Notebook view is set to "Page Width." To alter the view, launch Notebook and click on View. Go to Zoom and select the "Page Width" setting. If you use a screen display setting of 800 x 600 pixels, text in the prepared Notebook files may appear larger when you edit it on screen.

Getting started

The program should run automatically when you insert the CD-ROM into your CD drive. If it does not, use My Computer to browse to the contents of the CD-ROM and click on the Scholastic icon. (On the Mac, click on the Scholastic icon to start the program.)

Main menu

The Main menu divides the Notebook files by topic: Spelling & Vocabulary; Writing; Reading; and Grammar, Mechanics & Usage. Clicking on the appropriate button for any of these options will take you to a separate Lessons menu. (See below for further information.) The "Build Your Own" file is also accessed through the Main menu.

Individual Notebook files or pages can be located using the search facility by keying in words (or part of words) from the resource titles in the Search box. Press Go to begin the search. This will bring up a list of the titles that match your search.

Lessons menu

Each Lessons menu provides all of the prepared Notebook files for each chapter of the book. Click on the buttons to open the Notebook files. Click on Main menu button to return to the Main menu screen. (To alternate between the menus on the CD-ROM and other open applications, hold down the Alt key and press the Tab key to switch to the desired application.)

Safety note: Avoid looking directly at the projector beam as it is potentially damaging to the eyes, and never leave children unsupervised when using the interactive whiteboard.

Connections to the Common Core State Standards

The mini-lessons and activities in this book meet the following Common Core State Standards for English Language Arts:

SPELLING & VOCABULARY	
Plural Endings	**L.4.1, L.5.1, and L.6.1:** Demonstrate command of the conventions of standard English grammar and usage when writing or speaking.
Spelling Rules: "*i* before *e*"	**L.4.2, L.5.2, and L.6.2:** Demonstrate command of the conventions of standard English capitalization, punctuation, and spelling when writing.
Common Endings	**L.4.2, L.5.2, and L.6.2:** Demonstrate command of the conventions of standard English capitalization, punctuation, and spelling when writing.
Suffixes	**L.4.4b, L.5.4b, and L.6.4b:** Use common, grade-appropriate Greek and Latin affixes and roots as clues to the meaning of a word.
Prefixes	**L.4.4b, L.5.4b, and L.6.4b:** Use common, grade-appropriate Greek and Latin affixes and roots as clues to the meaning of a word.
Word Roots	**L.4.4b, L.5.4b, and L.6.4b:** Use common, grade-appropriate Greek and Latin affixes and roots as clues to the meaning of a word.
Word Building, Part 1	**L.4.4b, L.5.4b, and L.6.4b:** Use common, grade-appropriate Greek and Latin affixes and roots as clues to the meaning of a word.
Word Building, Part 2	**L.4.4b, L.5.4b, and L.6.4b:** Use common, grade-appropriate Greek and Latin affixes and roots as clues to the meaning of a word.
Homophones	n/a
WRITING	
Character Sketches	**W.4.3a and W.5.3a:** Orient the reader by establishing a situation and introducing a narrator and/or characters. **W.6.3a:** Engage and orient the reader by establishing a context and introducing a narrator and/or characters.
Story Planning	**W.4.3a and W.5.3a:** Orient the reader by establishing a situation and introducing a narrator and/or characters; organize an event sequence that unfolds naturally. **W.6.3a:** Engage and orient the reader by establishing a context and introducing a narrator and/or characters; organize an event sequence that unfolds naturally and logically.
Mapping Texts	**W.4.3a and W.5.3a:** Orient the reader by establishing a situation and introducing a narrator and/or characters; organize an event sequence that unfolds naturally. **W.4.3c:** Use a variety of transitional words and phrases to manage the sequence of events. **W.5.3c:** Use a variety of transitional words, phrases, and clauses to manage the sequence of events. **W.6.3a:** Engage and orient the reader by establishing a context and introducing a narrator and/or characters; organize an event sequence that unfolds naturally and logically. **W.6.3c:** Use a variety of transition words, phrases, and clauses to convey sequence and signal shifts from one time frame or setting to another.
Story Openings	**W.4.3a and W.5.3a:** Orient the reader by establishing a situation and introducing a narrator and/or characters; organize an event sequence that unfolds naturally. **W.6.3a:** Engage and orient the reader by establishing a context and introducing a narrator and/or characters; organize an event sequence that unfolds naturally and logically.
Direct and Indirect Speech	**W.4.3b:** Use dialogue and description to develop experiences and events or show the responses of characters to situations. **W.5.3b:** Use narrative techniques, such as dialogue, description, and pacing, to develop experiences and events or show the responses of characters to situations. **L.4.2b:** Use commas and quotation marks to mark direct speech and quotations from a text. **W.6.3b:** Use narrative techniques, such as dialogue, pacing, and description, to develop experiences, events, and/or characters.
Writing for an Audience	**W.4.4 and W.5.4:** Produce clear and coherent writing in which the development and organization are appropriate to task, purpose, and audience. **W.6.4:** Produce clear and coherent writing in which the development, organization, and style are appropriate to task, purpose, and audience.

Note-taking	**W.4.2 and W.5.2:** Write informative/explanatory texts to examine a topic and convey ideas and information clearly. **W.4.2a:** Introduce a topic clearly and group related information in paragraphs and sections; include formatting, illustrations, and multimedia when useful to aiding comprehension. **W.4.2b and W.5.2b:** Develop the topic with facts, definitions, concrete details, quotations, or other information and examples related to the topic. **W.4.2c:** Link ideas within categories of information using words and phrases. **W.4.2d, W.5.2d, and W.6.2d:** Use precise language and domain-specific vocabulary to inform about or explain the topic. **W.4.2e and W.5.2e:** Provide a concluding statement or section related to the information or explanation presented. **W.6.2a:** Introduce a topic; organize ideas, concepts, and information, using strategies such as definition, classification, comparison/contrast, and cause/effect; include formatting, graphics, and multimedia when useful to aiding comprehension. **W.6.2c:** Use appropriate transitions to clarify the relationships among ideas and concepts.
Instructional Texts	**W.4.2 and W.5.2:** Write informative/explanatory texts to examine a topic and convey ideas and information clearly. **L.4.3a:** Choose words and phrases to convey ideas precisely.
Summarizing	**RI.4.2:** Determine the main idea of a text and explain how it is supported by key details; summarize the text.
Complex Sentences	**L.4.1, L.5.1, and L.6.1:** Demonstrate command of the conventions of standard English grammar and usage when writing or speaking. **L.4.2c:** Use a comma before a coordinating conjunction in a compound sentence. **L.4.3a:** Choose words and phrases to convey ideas precisely. **L.4.3b:** Choose punctuation for effect. **L.5.2b:** Use a comma to separate an introductory element from the rest of the sentence. **L.5.3a:** Expand and combine sentences for meaning, reader/listener interest, and style. **L.6.3a:** Vary sentence patterns for meaning, reader/listener interest, and style.
Connecting Ideas	**W.4.1c:** Link opinion and reasons using words and phrases. **W.4.2c:** Link ideas within categories of information using words and phrases. **W.5.2c:** Link ideas within and across categories of information using words, phrases, and clauses. **W.6.2c:** Use appropriate transitions to clarify the relationships among ideas and concepts.
Paragraphs	**W.4.2a:** Introduce a topic clearly and group related information in paragraphs and sections; include formatting, illustrations, and multimedia when useful to aiding comprehension. **W.4.2b and W.5.2b:** Develop the topic with facts, definitions, concrete details, quotations, or other information and examples related to the topic. **W.4.2c:** Link ideas within categories of information using words and phrases. **W.4.2d, W.5.2d, and W.6.2d:** Use precise language and domain specific vocabulary to inform about or explain the topic.
Connecting Paragraphs	**W.4.2a:** Introduce a topic clearly and group related information in paragraphs and sections; include formatting, illustrations, and multimedia when useful to aiding comprehension. **W.4.2c:** Link ideas within categories of information using words and phrases. **W.4.2b and W.5.2b:** Develop the topic with facts, definitions, concrete details, quotations, or other information and examples related to the topic. **W.4.3a and W.5.3a:** Orient the reader by establishing a situation and introducing a narrator and/or characters; organize an event sequence that unfolds naturally. **W.4.3c:** Use a variety of transitional words and phrases to manage the sequence of events. **W.5.3c:** Use a variety of transitional words, phrases, and clauses to manage the sequence of events. **W.6.2c:** Use appropriate transitions to clarify the relationships among ideas and concepts. **W.6.3c:** Use a variety of transition words, phrases, and clauses to convey sequence and signal shifts from one time frame or setting to another.
Writing Narratives	**W.4.3 and W.5.3:** Write narratives to develop real or imagined experiences or events using effective technique, descriptive details, and clear event sequences. **W.6.3:** Write narratives to develop real or imagined experiences or events using effective technique, relevant descriptive details, and well-structured event sequences.
Persuasive Ads	**W.4.4 and W.5.4:** Produce clear and coherent writing in which the development and organization are appropriate to task, purpose, and audience. **W.6.4:** Produce clear and coherent writing in which the development, organization, and style are appropriate to task, purpose, and audience.
Writing Poetry	**W.4.3d and W.5.3d:** Use concrete words and phrases and sensory details to convey experiences and events precisely.
Imagery	**RL.5.4:** Determine the meaning of words and phrases as they are used in a text, including figurative language such as metaphors and similes. **L.4.5, L.5.5, and L.6.5:** Demonstrate understanding of figurative language, word relationships, and nuances in word meanings. **L.4.5a:** Explain the meaning of simple similes and metaphors in context. **L.5.5a:** Interpret figurative language, including similes and metaphors, in context.
Similes, Metaphors & Personification	**RL.5.4:** Determine the meaning of words and phrases as they are used in a text, including figurative language such as metaphors and similes. **L.4.5, L.5.5, and L.6.5:** Demonstrate understanding of figurative language, word relationships, and nuances in word meanings. **L.4.5a:** Explain the meaning of simple similes and metaphors in context. **L.5.5a:** Interpret figurative language, including similes and metaphors, in context. **L.6.5a:** Interpret figures of speech (e.g., personification) in context.

READING	
Idioms	**L.4.5b and L.5.5b:** Recognize and explain the meaning of common idioms, adages, and proverbs.
Reading Journals	**RL.4.2:** Determine a theme of a story, drama, or poem from details in the text; summarize the text.
Making Notes	**RI.4.2:** Determine the main idea of a text and explain how it is supported by key details; summarize the text. **RI.5.2:** Determine the two or more main ideas of a text and explain how they are supported by key details; summarize the text. **RI.6.2:** Determine a central idea of a text and analyze its development over the course of the text, including how it emerges and is shaped and refined by specific details; provide an objective summary of the text.
Point of View	**RL.4.6:** Compare and contrast the point of view from which different stories are narrated, including the difference between first- and third-person narrations. **RL.5.6:** Describe how a narrator's or speaker's point of view influences how events are described. **RL.6.6:** Explain how an author develops the point of view of the narrator or speaker in a text.
Myths	**RL.4.2:** Determine a theme of a story, drama, or poem from details in the text; summarize the text. **RL.4.4:** Determine the meaning of words and phrases as they are used in a text, including those that allude to significant characters found in mythology. **RL.5.2:** Determine a theme of a story, drama, or poem from details in the text, including how characters in a story or drama respond to challenges or how the speaker in a poem reflects upon a topic; summarize the text. **RL.6.3:** Describe how a particular story's or drama's plot unfolds in a series of episodes as well as how the characters respond or change as the plot moves toward a resolution.
Fables	**RL.4.2:** Determine a theme of a story, drama, or poem from details in the text; summarize the text.
Poetry & Words	**RL.4.2:** Determine a theme of a story, drama, or poem from details in the text; summarize the text. **RL.5.2:** Determine a theme of a story, drama, or poem from details in the text, including how characters in a story or drama respond to challenges or how the speaker in a poem reflects upon a topic; summarize the text. **RF.4.4b and RF.5.4b:** Read on-level prose and poetry orally with accuracy, appropriate rate, and expression on successive readings.
Reading Narratives	**RL.5.9:** Compare and contrast stories in the same genre (e.g., adventure stories) on their approaches to similar themes and topics. **RL.6.4:** Determine the meaning of words and phrases as they are used in a text, including figurative and connotative meanings; analyze the impact of a specific word choice on meaning and tone.
Nonfiction Texts	**RI.4.5:** Describe the overall structure of events, ideas, concepts, or information in a text or part of a text. **RI.5.5:** Compare and contrast the overall structure of events, ideas, concepts, or information in two or more texts. **RI.6.5:** Analyze how a particular sentence, paragraph, chapter, or section fits into the overall structure of a text and contributes to the development of ideas. **RI.6.6:** Determine an author's point of view or purpose in a text and explain how it is conveyed in the text.
Book Review	**RL.4.2:** Determine a theme of a story, drama, or poem from details in the text; summarize the text. **RL.4.3:** Describe in depth a character, setting, or event in a story or drama, drawing on specific details in the text. **RL.5.2:** Determine a theme of a story, drama, or poem from details in the text, including how characters in a story or drama respond to challenges or how the speaker in a poem reflects upon a topic; summarize the text. **W.4.1 and W.5.1:** Write opinion pieces on topics or texts, supporting a point of view with reasons and information. **W.6.1:** Write arguments to support claims with clear reasons and relevant evidence.
GRAMMAR, MECHANICS, & USAGE	
Verbs and Tenses	**L.4.1, L.5.1, and L.6.1:** Demonstrate command of the conventions of standard English grammar and usage when writing or speaking. **L.5.1c:** Use verb tense to convey various times, sequences, states, and conditions. **L.5.1d:** Recognize and correct inappropriate shifts in verb tense.
Adverbs	**L.4.1, L.5.1, and L.6.1:** Demonstrate command of the conventions of standard English grammar and usage when writing or speaking.
Adjectives	**L.4.1, L.5.1, and L.6.1:** Demonstrate command of the conventions of standard English grammar and usage when writing or speaking.
Parts of Speech, Part 1	**L.4.1, L.5.1, and L.6.1:** Demonstrate command of the conventions of standard English grammar and usage when writing or speaking.
Parts of Speech, Part 2	**L.4.1, L.5.1, and L.6.1:** Demonstrate command of the conventions of standard English grammar and usage when writing or speaking.
Prepositions	**L.4.1, L.5.1, and L.6.1:** Demonstrate command of the conventions of standard English grammar and usage when writing or speaking.
Word Order	**L.4.1, L.5.1, and L.6.1:** Demonstrate command of the conventions of standard English grammar and usage when writing or speaking. **L.4.3a:** Choose words and phrases to convey ideas precisely.
Passive & Active Voices	**L.4.1, L.5.1, and L.6.1:** Demonstrate command of the conventions of standard English grammar and usage when writing or speaking. **L.4.3 and L.5.3:** Use knowledge of language and its conventions when writing, speaking, reading, or listening.
Apostrophes & Possession	**L.4.2, L.5.2, and L.6.2:** Demonstrate command of the conventions of standard English capitalization, punctuation, and spelling when writing.
Its and *It's*	**L.4.2, L.5.2, and L.6.2:** Demonstrate command of the conventions of standard English capitalization, punctuation, and spelling when writing.
Punctuation	**L.4.2, L.5.2, and L.6.2:** Demonstrate command of the conventions of standard English capitalization, punctuation, and spelling when writing.

Plural Endings

Learning objective
- To know and apply common spelling rules.

Resources
- "Plural Endings" Notebook file
- "A Strange Shopping List" (p. 59)
- writing notebooks and pens

Whiteboard tools
- Eraser
- Pen tray
- Highlighter pen
- Select tool

Getting Started

Display page 2 of the "Plural Endings" Notebook file and ask students to write in the plural forms for the first three words. Use the Eraser from the Pen tray to reveal the answers on the right and highlight the suffixes that form the plural. Do the same for the next three words. Then extend the work to plurals where *-s* is not added by repeating the activity for the next group of words on page 3.

Mini-Lesson

1. Go to page 4 of the Notebook file. Pair up students. Have one partner read the word in the left-hand column of the table, then the other partner say its plural form. Have them agree on the pronunciation of the plural.
2. Discuss the plurals with the class. If there is dispute, encourage students to use the answers in sentences. Can they now hear which sounds correct?
3. Invite students to write the plural of each word in the central column. Check if the answer is right each time, using the Eraser.
4. When the table is complete, ask students to study the words and to figure out a spelling rule for converting these words from singular to plural.
5. Share ideas and write a list on the next page:
   - Words ending in *-f*, change to *-ves* to make them plural.
   - Words ending in *-ff*, add *-s* to make them plural.
   - Words ending in *-fe*, change to *-ves* to make them plural.
6. Investigate which rule applies to each word in the table on page 4.
7. Write the word *chief* under the rules on page 5. Ask: *Which rule should we apply?* (You would expect to use rule 1.) *What will the plural be?* (Chieves) *Does it sound correct?* (No)
8. Explain that the correct plural is *chiefs*. Spelling rules cannot always be applied. There are many exceptions. Demonstrate how a dictionary can help with problem words.

Independent Work

Ask students to complete "A Strange Shopping List" (p. 59). Divide the words into groups for less-confident learners. As an extra challenge, ask students to add more text, using other *-ff*, *-f*, and *-fe* words and their plural forms.

Wrap-Up

Work through the reproducible sheet together and compare students' answers with the answers on pages 6 and 7 of the Notebook file. Invite students to write the answer you agree upon. Show the correct plural forms by deleting the stars on the right-hand side of pages 6 and 7. (Draw attention to *scarf*: the plural can be *scarfs* or *scarves*.) Share some of students' spells from their reproducible sheets.

Spelling Rules: "*i* before *e*"

Learning objective
- To group and classify words according to their spelling patterns.

Resources
- "Spelling Rules" Notebook file
- individual whiteboards and pens
- computers, if available

Whiteboard tools
- Pen tray
- Select tool
- Delete button
- Fill Color tool

Getting Started

Go to page 2 of the "Spelling Rules" Notebook file. Tell students to write on individual whiteboards one thing that the words have in common and one thing that they don't. Have them compare answers with a partner. Encourage them to look closely at spelling and to say the words to each other. Share ideas as a class and identify the common feature (they all contain *ie*) and the difference (*ie* has a different pronunciation each time). Pull out the tabs to check that students are correct.

Mini-Lesson

1. The letters *i* and *e* are often next to each other in words. Ask: *Which order is more common—*ie *or* ei? (*ie*)
2. Ask students to write any *ie* word (not a Getting Started example) on their individual whiteboards. Count the number of different words.
3. Go to page 3 of the Notebook file and remove the box covering the heading of the first column, *ie*, using the Delete button or selecting the Delete option from the drop-down menu. List students' words underneath.
4. Ask: *Which letter makes words break the* ie *spelling rule?* (*c*) Tell students the spelling rule: i *before* e *except after* c.
5. Delete the box covering the heading of the second column, *cei*. Six words are listed but concealed in the column. Reveal each word's letters gradually by pulling back the box covering them, encouraging students to predict spelling and words.
6. Say the word *vein*. Emphasize its long-a sound. Explain that *ei* makes this sound. Delete the box over the next column heading, *ei* (long-a sound), and give clues to allow students to predict words and their spelling. Reveal the words in the column.
7. Some words simply break the rules and these are best memorized. Delete the box over the final heading, *ei* (other sounds), and gradually reveal the words in the column. Assign these words as homework.

Independent Work

Ask students to design and create a poster advertising the *i* and *e* spelling pattern. Suggest that each poster concentrate on one or two rules. Some students could design and complete their poster on the computer.

Allow less-confident learners to work in pairs. Ask more-confident learners to find *ie* words on three pages of their reading book. They should group the words they find according to the way *ie* sounds.

Wrap-Up

Scan, upload, and view students' posters on page 4 of the Notebook file. Ask students to explain the information to the rest of the class. Encourage constructive feedback. Play the spelling game on pages 5 and 6.

Common Endings

Learning objective

- To know and apply common spelling rules.

Resources

- "Common Endings" Notebook file
- "Common Endings Crossword" (p. 60)
- individual white-boards and pens

Whiteboard tools

- Pen tray
- Select tool
- Delete button

Getting Started

Say *tough*, *fiction*, and *trivial* out loud and ask students to spell the words on their individual whiteboards. Open the "Common Endings" Notebook file and go to page 2. Compare students' spellings. Explain that these words are difficult to spell. Can students suggest ways to remember the spellings? Share ideas. These may include: pronunciation and letter sounds; common letter strings; the number of syllables in a word; typical patterns of letter strings; a mnemonic. As students suggest a way of remembering, encourage them to explain it.

Mini-Lesson

1. Display page 3 of the Notebook file. Explain that the bag contains words that are commonly misspelled. Drag the words out of the bag and read them together.
2. Ask students to sort the words into groups on their individual whiteboards. Allow them time to think before comparing ideas of how the words could be sorted.
3. Delete the white box to reveal a table. Place *devious* in one column. Encourage students to suggest other words that could go in the same group, and why. Guide them to recognize that *devious*, *serious*, and *obvious* are similar because of their endings (*-ious*). Invite students to move the words together in one column and write in the heading *-ious*.
4. In the same way, work with students to create groups for these word endings: *-ial*, *-tion*, *-ight*, *-ough*.
5. Read aloud the *-ough* words. Ask students if they notice anything strange about this group of words. Repeat the words if necessary, until students focus on pronunciation (*-ough* makes a different sound in each word). Explain that *-ough* is the most unpredictable of these five words endings: it can have a number of different pronunciations.
6. Focus on the *-ial* group. In these three words, highlight the letter preceding *-ial*. Point out that these words are typical: the letter preceding *-ial* is usually *c* or *t*.
7. Talk about parts of speech. *What part of speech are the* -tion *words?* (Noun) *Which other group is made up of nouns?* (*-ight*) *Which endings usually belong to adjectives?* (*-ial* and *-ious*) *Which group is most likely to vary?* (*-ough*)

Independent Work

Ask students to complete the crossword on page 60. Emphasize the need to think about spelling. Write the common endings of the words used on the SMART Board, if you think students need this support (*-ial*, *-ight*, *-ough*, *-ious*, *-tion*).

Supply less-confident learners with the initial letters of answers. As an extra challenge, ask more-confident learners to list their answers, finding ways to group them according to pronunciation, part of speech, and spelling patterns.

Wrap-Up

Display the crossword on page 4 of the Notebook file. Invite students to come up and fill in the crossword. Press the Clues button to read the clues (if required) and the Answers button to see a completed version of the crossword. Identify common spelling patterns and write them on page 5.

Suffixes

Learning objective
- To learn how to recognize and spell words with the suffixes *-ship*, *-hood*, *-ment*, *-ness*, and more.

Resources
- "Suffixes" Notebook file
- individual whiteboards and pens
- printed copy of page 5 of the Notebook file for each student

Whiteboard tools
- Pen tray
- Select tool
- Highlighter pen

Getting Started

Display page 2 of the "Suffixes" Notebook file. Discuss how to sort the words, eventually moving them so that they are grouped like this:

- Group 1: *champion, member, owner, neighbor*
- Group 2: *partnership, childhood, ownership*

Explain that the words in Group 1 are root words and the words in Group 2 are made from root words plus additional letters. Show students how *owner* and *ownership* make a pair. Ask volunteers to supply the missing word to pair with the root words on the page. (*champion—championship; member—membership; neighbor—neighborhood; partner—partnership; child—childhood*)

Mini-Lesson

1. Explain that a *suffix* is a group of letters added to the end of a word. Each root word in the Getting Started uses a suffix to become another word.
2. Focus on the suffix *-ship*. Talk about words ending this way, such as *fellowship* or *partnership*. Write them on page 3 of the Notebook file. Ask students to highlight the root words.
3. Discuss how the suffix affects the meaning of the new word. Encourage the class to think about what *-ship* means in these words. Establish that it is a way of living or a skill.
4. Display page 4 of the Notebook file. Point to a root word and ask students to choose a suffix for it, writing *a* or *b* on their individual whiteboards.
5. Ask volunteers to drag the words into the correct boxes. Note that *silly* does not work in either, although *silliness* is a valid word. Point out that the addition of a suffix can alter the spelling of the root word: if the root word ends in *y*, the *y* usually changes to *i* when a suffix is added.
6. Reverse the activity, looking at the new, extended word and identifying the original, root word.

Independent Work

Print out a copy of page 5 of the Notebook page for each child. Students must choose a suffix for each root word, listing the root word and the new word in the correct column. Encourage students to use dictionaries for their investigation.

Reduce the list of root words and limit the choice of suffixes to two for less-confident learners. As an extra challenge, ask more-confident learners to make their own additions to the columns.

Wrap-Up

Display page 5 of the Notebook page and invite students to drag the words into the table. Note the words that do not work because of spelling changes. Encourage students to suggest other words that could be added to the lists. Use page 6 to work together on lists of words for the suffixes *-dom, -ance, -ence, -ation, -ology*.

Prefixes

Learning objective

- To know and use less common prefixes, such as *im-* and *ir-*.

Resources

- "Prefixes" Notebook file
- "Irresistible Crossword" (p. 61)
  - individual whiteboards and pens

Whiteboard tools

- Pen tray
- Delete button
- Fill Color tool
- Select tool

Getting Started

Remind students of the terms *synonym* (a word of the same meaning) and *antonym* (a word of the opposite meaning). Go to page 2 of the "Prefixes" Notebook file. Use the Delete button to uncover a word hidden behind an oval. Say the word out loud. Give students ten seconds to write a synonym on their whiteboards. Do this for five words, then ask students to hold up their whiteboards. Compare answers and repeat the exercise for the antonyms.

Mini-Lesson

1. Read the words on page 3 of the Notebook file. Ask students to use them orally in sentences. Discuss what the words mean.
2. Ask students to write an antonym for each word on their individual whiteboards. Compare results. Check to see if any students have used a prefix in front of the original word.
3. Explain that the most accurate antonyms can be made with prefixes. Reveal the antonyms on page 3. Highlight the prefixes.
4. Ask: *What do the prefixes mean?* (Not) *Can you think of other prefixes that mean "not"?* (*ir-*, *im-*, *un-*, *dis-*, *de-*, *anti-*)
5. Return to your Getting Started words. Add relevant prefixes in front of the words to form antonyms.
6. Go to page 4. Form antonyms by using one of the prefixes shown. Allow time for students to decide and write answers on their individual whiteboards. Ask them to hold up their answers before you drag and drop the word into its correct circle where the appropriate prefix is attached.
7. Investigate the words in each circle. Point out patterns:
   - *il-* is used in front of words starting with *l*
   - *im-* goes before words starting with *m* or *p*
   - *ir-* goes in front of words starting with *r*
8. Emphasize the spelling patterns of double letters. Point out that words can show the same spelling patterns, but not have the root meaning of "not," for example: *illuminate*, *illustrate*, *irritate*, *irrigate*.

Independent Work

Give out copies of "Irresistible Crossword" (p. 61) for students to complete. Suggest checking spelling in a dictionary. (Answers are on p. 5 of the Notebook file.)

Wrap-Up

Point out that many of the clues relate to the prefix by using the word *not*. Talk about the meanings of other prefixes, such as *sus-* and *pro-*. List some words with these prefixes, like *suspicion*, *suspend*, *projection*. Ask: *What do you think the prefixes mean?* (*sus-* [like *sub-*] means "under"; *pro-* means "ahead"). Use pages 5, 6, and 7 of the Notebook file to assess students' understanding of prefixes that mean "not."

Word Roots

Learning objective

- To use knowledge of word structures and origins to develop an understanding of word meanings.

Resources

- "Word Roots" Notebook file
- "Word Webs" (p. 62)
- dictionaries

Whiteboard tools

- Pen tray
- Screen Shade
- Select tool
- Lines tool

Getting Started

Look at page 2 of the "Word Roots" Notebook file. Allow students time to think about what the words have in common. Explain that they have a common root. Use a Highlighter pen to identify the root (*mono*). Explain that it is from the Greek word for "alone." Use dictionaries to define the words, using *alone* in the definitions. Ask students if they can add a word to your collection. Make sure that the meaning of a new word relates to the meaning of the root.

Mini-Lesson

1. Display page 3 of the Notebook file. Explain that you are going to show students some sentences containing words with a common root. Move the Screen Shade to reveal the sentences one at a time. Allow time for students to think about each sentence and to write the words on their individual whiteboards. Compare answers before highlighting the two words.
2. Investigate the identified words. Ask: *What is the root?* Underline the roots.
3. Investigate further by asking students to use dictionaries to find the meaning and origin of each root. Make sure that they recognize how the meaning of the root affects the meaning of the word.
4. Go to page 4 of the Notebook file and press on the image to open the "Common Roots" activity. Explain the page: each definition must be matched to a root word.
5. Pair up students and allow them time to think and discuss before agreeing on an answer. Invite students to come to the SMART Board to match the roots and labels. Check answers by pressing "Am I correct?" The answers are given on page 5.
6. On page 6, make a word web together for one of the roots from the Notebook file. (Use the Lines tool to add extra lines if necessary.)

Independent Work

Ask students to complete the "Word Webs" on page 62. Encourage the use of a dictionary, but remind students to check the meanings of the words they use.

Reduce the number of spaces to fill in for each web to support less-confident learners. As an extra challenge, ask students to add another word or two to each web.

Wrap-Up

Use pages 7 to 14 of the Notebook file to go over the independent work. Invite students to fill in the webs with the words they have found. Use page 15 to check students' answers and to see some examples of words that contain the relevant roots.

Word Building, Part 1

Learning objective

- To employ a range of strategies to spell difficult and unfamiliar words.

Resources

- "Word Building, Part 1" Notebook file
- "Word Clusters" (p. 63)
- individual whiteboards and pens

Whiteboard tools

- Pen tray
- Delete button
- Select tool
- On-screen Keyboard

Getting Started

Page 2 of the "Word Building, Part 1" Notebook file shows a circle with *pro* written in the middle. Ask students to list, on their individual whiteboards, words containing *pro* (for example: *professor*, *proceed*, *proactive*, *project*). Write some of students' examples in the circle.

Mini-Lesson

1. Go to page 3 of the Notebook file and give students two minutes to list words with *super* in them (for example: *superb*, *superficial*, *superhero*, *supermarket*). Compare results, writing words in the circle.
2. Ask students to consider what the word *super* means. Delete the panel to reveal the answer ("above"). Explain that in this context *above* means "greater." Which of students' words belong in this circle? (Words with the same spelling and meaning) Check if any now have to be deleted.
3. Encourage students to define the words, using the word *above*. Do the same with the *pro* ("before") circle on the previous page.
4. Repeat the activity with the word *prim* on page 4 (for example: *primary*, *primrose*, *primitive*, *primate*).
5. Go to page 5. Explain that *tri* is a Greek and Latin prefix that means "three." Delete the panels to reveal the answers. Challenge students to write a *tri* word on their whiteboards. Ask them to show their answers and write some examples in the yellow triangle.
6. Repeat the activity on page 6 for *re*.
7. Go to page 7 and explain that students must find the words to fit the meaning clues. There is a mixture of prefixes, suffixes, and roots that can be combined to build the words.
8. Allow students time to think about each clue and to write words on their individual whiteboards. Discuss answers before dragging and dropping the labels into place, next to their clues, to form the words.
9. Underline or highlight the word parts in different colors. Encourage students to explain what each part means. Compare answers, before deleting the red rectangle, then erasing the green ones beneath to reveal the meanings of the word parts.

Independent Work

Provide each child with a copy of "Word Clusters" (p. 63). Students should complete the word clusters, writing a word on each petal that uses the root in the flower center. The new words must contain both the root's meaning and letters.

Wrap-Up

Use pages 8 and 9 of the Notebook file to discuss the work that students completed during independent work. Encourage students to share their answers and annotate the petals with their words.

Word Building, Part 2

Learning objective

- To employ a range of strategies to spell difficult and unfamiliar words.

Resources

- "Word Building, Part 2" Notebook file
- "Unusual People" (p. 64)
- individual whiteboards and pens
- writing materials
- computers (optional)

Whiteboard tools

- Pen tray
- Select tool
- Highlighter pen
- Delete button
- On-screen Keyboard

Getting Started

Go to page 2 of the "Word Building, Part 2" Notebook file. Ask students to choose ten difficult words from two pages of their reading books and write them on their individual whiteboards. Then invite them to exchange boards with a partner and write (in one word) a meaning for the words listed. Encourage students to compare results, checking their answers in a dictionary and discussing the construction of each word.

Mini-Lesson

1. Go to page 3 of the Notebook file. Talk about word building, reminding students that new words can be constructed from a combination of prefixes, suffixes, and roots.
2. Demonstrate with the word *conclude* on the SMART Board. Use the Select tool to deconstruct the word into: *con* + *clude*. Ask: *Which is the root word?* (*clude*) *What is* con? (A prefix)
3. Ask students to suggest other words using the same root word (such as *preclude*, *include*, and *exclude*). Share results, writing them on the SMART Board. Use the meanings of these words to help students work out the meaning of the root word. (Shut)
4. Allow partner discussion time as students investigate the meanings of the prefixes. Suggest thinking of other words with the same prefix. Write the meanings on the SMART Board: *pre* = before; *in* = within; *con* = together; *ex* = outside.
5. Explain the game on page 4: Students must combine word parts to create a word to fit a meaning clue. Challenge the partners to identify and write the words on their individual whiteboards within a few minutes.
6. Demonstrate constructing the answers by dragging and dropping the word parts into the orange rectangles. Focus on the separate word parts, underlining or highlighting them in different colors.
7. Move on to page 5 and organize students into two teams to play another game. Teams take turns to give the correct meaning for a word part. They could designate a representative to either come to the board to write their meaning in a column, or to say the meaning for you to scribe. One point is awarded for a correct answer. Reveal the answer only when the team's answer is correct.
8. Display page 6. Point out the word *arachnophobia*. Discuss its make up and what each part means: *arachna* (spider) + *phobia* (fear). Have fun by combining word parts to invent new words. For example, *vacca* = cows; *phobia* = fear. Put them together for *vaccaphobia*! (An invented word for "fear of cows")

Independent Work

Invite students to invent new words to complete the poems in "Unusual People" (p. 64). Discuss the words and their meanings. Use the space on page 7 of the Notebook file to write invented words and their meanings to provide further support for students in this task.

Wrap-Up

Choose students to type or write their poems on page 8 of the Notebook file. Encourage them to define the invented words.

Homophones

Learning objective
- To distinguish the spelling and meaning of common homophones.

Resources
- "Homophones" Notebook file
- "Letter to Mom" (p. 65)
- individual whiteboards and pens

Whiteboard tools
- Pen tray
- Highlighter pen
- Select tool
- Delete button

Getting Started

Look at page 2 of the "Homophones" Notebook file. Ask students what the three words in the pictures have in common. *(They are pronounced the same way.)* Point out that although they are said the same way, they are spelled differently.

Explain that you want to sort the words on page 3 into small groups by playing "Sound Snap." Drag one word into one of the circles, and ask a volunteer to identify another word that sounds the same. If the answer is wrong, the turn passes to someone else. If correct, say "Snap" and drag the matching word to the circle. Some of the words are in groups of three. In these cases, highlight a word in a circle for students to guess the third one of the group. Keep going until all the words are in circles.

Mini-Lesson

1. Point to the word *Homophone* on page 4 of the Notebook file. Ask students what they think it means. Reveal the definition behind the red box.
2. Explain that the words they played "Sound Snap" with are homophones. Encourage students to suggest other examples and add them to page 3 in the remaining circles.
3. Play "Solve My Riddle" by asking students to tell you which word on page 3 fits the clue, for example:
   - I am very wet. *(sea)*
   - I am one more than three. *(four)*
   - I say "baa." *(ewe)*

   Allow partner collaboration and thinking time as students write their answers on individual whiteboards. Highlight words as they are identified. Encourage students to make up some riddles of their own.
4. Discuss whether students confuse particular homophones. Ask: *How do you remember the correct one?* Share helpful memory tips.
5. Display page 5 of the Notebook file. Work together to invent *mnemonics*—devices to aid memory.

Independent Work

Give each child a copy of "Letter to Mom" (p. 65). Explain that the Roman soldier, writing a letter from Britain, has all the words he needs in the box. Students must decide which word goes where.

Advise less-confident learners which set of homophones to choose from. As an extra challenge, encourage more-confident learners to compose their own letter containing between 10 and 15 deliberate mistakes. Can someone else spot the mistakes?

Wrap-Up

Display page 6 of the Notebook file. Discuss possible answers before allowing students to drag the correct words from the homophones box into the text. Delete incorrect words. Pull the screen across the text to reveal the correct answers.

Character Sketches

Learning objective
- To use characterization to engage readers' interest.

Resources
- "Character Sketches" Notebook file

Whiteboard tools
- Pen tray
- Select tool

Getting Started

Display page 2 of the "Character Sketches" Notebook file. Read the text and discuss it. Ask students to vote whether they like or dislike Father and Mother. Discuss the results. Highlight parts of the text that could have affected feelings (not wanting to share, not being rich, the word *schemed*).

Mini-Lesson

1. Display page 3 of the Notebook file. Discuss the events of the text (Aled's actions, dragons coming by sea).
2. Focus on the character Aled. Ask: *What sort of person do you think he is? How can you tell? Do you like or dislike him? Why?* Encourage discussion and different viewpoints, emphasizing that people respond to writing differently.
3. Point out specific details from the passage. Discuss each of the details in turn, asking students to think about how the words make them feel about Aled (for example, "He got rid of all signs of his presence" might show that Aled has a careful nature).
4. Ask students whether the words add information about the character. Does it make them feel more sympathetic toward him? Does one detail make them dislike Aled? Encourage varied viewpoints.
5. If required, draw out details from the text by double-clicking on the text, then highlighting the words you want to isolate and dragging them out of the text box. This adds the words to the page as a separate object.
6. Focus on the verbs the writer has chosen. Ask: *Are they good choices?* (The verbs are often weak and there is repetition.) Make the point that more powerful verbs could improve this passage. Highlight some weak verbs in the first two lines.
7. Print a copy of the text for every student.

Independent Work

Ask students to read the text by themselves. Encourage them to highlight at least 15 verbs that need to be replaced. They should then replace them with powerful verbs.

Support less-confident learners by focusing on a smaller number of replacements of the weakest verbs (*put*, *saw*, *got*). As an extra challenge, ask more-confident learners to write the next part of the story, using powerful verbs and small details to evoke more sympathy or dislike of Aled.

Wrap-Up

Have students write their replacement verbs on the copy of the text on page 4 of the Notebook file. Discuss the effect more powerful verbs have on audience reaction. Return to the original version on page 3 so that other students can write alternative verbs. There is a text using stronger verbs on page 5 of the Notebook file, but other verbs are, of course, possible.

Story Planning

Learning objective
- To organize text into paragraphs to distinguish between different information, events, or processes.

Resources
- "Story Planning" Notebook file
- "Story Planner" (p. 66)
- individual whiteboards and pens
- writing notebooks

Whiteboard tools
- Eraser
- Pen tray
- Select tool
- Area Capture tool

Getting Started

Display page 2 of the "Story Planning" Notebook file. Read the text and ask students what they notice about it. (The narrative is not in the correct sequence.) Invite students to change the paragraph order. When you have agreed on a correct sequence, use the Eraser to rub over the circles to reveal the correct order.

Mini-Lesson

1. Discuss paragraphs, making notes on page 3 of the Notebook file. Explain that paragraphs mark different stages in the story—they help writers organize their thoughts and readers to follow the story line.
2. Explain that paragraphs can vary in length: The introduction and the ending to a story are often shorter than other paragraphs.
3. Go to page 4 and open the "Story Planning" activity. Discuss the picture sequence. Ask: *What do you think is happening? Which events are important? Is there a main character?*
4. Ask students what is wrong with the pictures. (They are in the wrong order.) Challenge them to decide and note on their individual whiteboards what the picture order should be.
5. Discuss their answers and agree on an order. Move the frames into the correct sequence. How does it compare with their individual whiteboard suggestions? Were there points students had not thought about?
6. Take a snapshot of the correct story sequence using the Area Capture tool and add it to the Notebook page. (To upload scanned images, select Insert, then Picture File, and browse to where you have saved the image.)
7. Suggest that each picture represents a paragraph. Annotate each picture with a planning sentence. Write these stage names next to the pictures, discussing each one as you do so:

   a. introduction
   b. build-up
   c. climax
   d. resolution
   e. ending

8. Go to page 5 of the Notebook file. Ask students to plan another story about the evacuees, using the stages that have been discussed.

Independent Work

Have students plan their stories on the "Story Planner" (p. 66) and write the opening paragraph on their writing notebooks.

Wrap-Up

Scan in and view some of students' plans and opening paragraphs. Discuss the progression. Use page 6 of the Notebook file to write the sequence of events in some of the story plans. Listen to some of the students read their introductions and discuss as a class how effective they are. Use an extended writing session to finish the story.

Mapping Texts

Learning objective

- To experiment with different narrative forms and styles to write original stories.

Resources

- "Mapping Texts" Notebook file
- "Mapping Texts" (p. 67)
- writing materials

Whiteboard tools

- Pen tray
- Select tool
- Fill Color tool
- Lines tool

Getting Started

Discuss with students what methods they use to plan stories—for example, storyboards, graphic organizers, mind maps, and notes. Make notes on page 2 of the Notebook file.

Mini-Lesson

1. Point out that stories do not always contain one narrative—sometimes two narratives (perhaps set in different times or in different places) are woven into one story. Careful planning is even more important when writing this kind of story.
2. Ask: *What would the writer have to consider?* Write suggestions on page 3 of the Notebook file. Ask: *How will the story be divided between the two narratives? In what order will the two narratives be dealt with? How will the two narratives come together?*
3. Go to page 4 and display the graphic organizer. Ask: *Which characters have a narrative?* Point out the two orange boxes on the left. Ask: *In what order will the writer plan to relate the narratives?* (Alternately) Discuss why it is not a good idea to tell one narrative first and then to tell the other.
4. Fill the boxes and talk about the contents of each box, one at a time. Each box briefly summarizes what that paragraph or section will be about. Use the Lines tool to draw arrows to emphasize:
   - how the story alternates between the narratives, shifting between characters and places (different places in the forest);
   - the way the two narratives are drawn together at the end.
5. Discuss different narratives that can be used in stories. For example: reality versus a dream; the present versus the past. On page 5 of the Notebook file, write examples of stories and the types of narratives that are used.
6. Go to page 6. Discuss the ways in which writers move smoothly from one narrative to another (for example, with transition words and new paragraphs) and write down ideas. The writer has to use interesting and varied ways to "flag" these narrative changes. Warn students against repeating overused phrases, such as "Meanwhile at the . . ."

Independent Work

Give out copies of "Mapping Texts" (p. 67) and ask students to plan the story of Cinderella (traditional or their own version). Their story should have two narratives that meet at the end.

Wrap-Up

Complete the table on page 7 of the Notebook file to review one child's plan for the story. Discuss other story plans. Does the rest of the class understand the plans? Talk about the transitions that could be used to move between the two narratives.

Story Openings

Learning objective
- To analyze the features of a good opening and compare a number of story openings.

Resources
- "Story Openings" Notebook file
- writing materials

Whiteboard tools
- Pen tray
- Select tool
- Highlighter pen

Getting Started

Discuss the importance of a story's opening: It is the writer's chance to "hook" the reader. Ask students to suggest some examples of good story openings and discuss these. Write their comments on page 2 of the "Story Openings" Notebook file.

Mini-Lesson

1. Read the opening of your current class novel. Ask: *Do you want to read on?* Encourage students to give reasons for their answers. Read other story openings and ask students to evaluate them, giving reasons for their opinions.
2. Discuss some reasons why openings may succeed:
   - funny or unusual descriptions (for example, *Matilda* by Roald Dahl)
   - details to arouse your interest in the characters (for example, *Maniac Magee* by Jerry Spinelli)
   - characters with wide appeal (for example, *The Hundred and One Dalmatians* by Dodie Smith)
3. Go to page 3 of the Notebook file. Agree on a class list of important features for story openings. Press the button to reveal a list of "Important features for story openings." Add any features that students have not identified by highlighting the text and dragging it onto page 3 in the Page Sorter.
4. Go to page 4 of the Notebook file. Ask for students' opinions of this story opening. Investigate the text closely, identifying examples of the features listed. For example:
   a. Answers important questions:
      - *Who?* Bennie, Kurt, Dad
      - *Where?* Computer laboratory
      - *When?* At night

   b. Uses expressive language: *almost controls you*; *lost his nerve*; *extraordinary*

   c. Introduces intrigue/questions: *Whose voice is it? What does this game do?*
5. Explain that students are going to write their own story opening. Suggest possible themes linked to a different curriculum area, such as:
   - A moving toy shows strange powers.
   - An archaeological dig unearths a piece of ancient Greek pottery. Myths and legends are linked to the pottery.

Independent Work

Encourage students to write their story opening. Emphasize that they must make the reader want to read more. Support less-confident learners by helping with planning and setting the scene.

Wrap-Up

Invite students to read their story openings aloud. Does the audience (the class) want to find out more? Write good opening sentences on the Notebook page.

Direct and Indirect Speech

Learning objectives
- To vary the pace and develop the viewpoint through the use of direct and indirect speech.
- To adapt sentence structure to different text-types, purposes, and readers.
- To punctuate sentences accurately, including use of quotation marks.

Resources
- "Direct and Indirect Speech" Notebook file
- writing materials

Whiteboard tools
- Pen tool
- Select tool
- On-screen Keyboard
- Highlighter pen

Getting Started

Read through page 2 of the "Direct and Indirect Speech" Notebook file. Ask what students notice about the two texts. They should realize that both tell the same story but are presented differently: (a) uses the actual words spoken; (b) reports the words that were spoken. Pull out the tabs to reveal this.

Mini-Lesson

1. Use and define the terms *direct speech* and *indirect speech*:
   a. *Direct speech* uses the speaker's original words.
   b. *Indirect speech* does not quote the original words of the speaker.
2. Go to page 3. Use a Highlighter pen to highlight the sentence: *"Will you do me a favor, Red Riding Hood?" she asked.* Ask students to identify the equivalent sentence in (b) and highlight it in the same color.
3. Repeat this for the other direct speech sentences. Use different colors for each pair of sentences.
4. Investigate the differences between the direct and indirect speech:
   - verb tense (*Will* becomes *would*)
   - person (*you* becomes *she*)
   - subordinating words (*if* is added)
   - word order (*Will you* changes to *she would*)
   - punctuation (? becomes .)
5. Demonstrate differences between *"I'd love to," answered Red Riding Hood* and *Red Riding Hood said that she would love to go*:
   - verb tense (*I'd* becomes *she would*)
   - person (*I* becomes *she*)
   - subordinating words (*that* is added)
6. Focus on *that*. Explain that the word *that* is often omitted but the meaning of the sentence remains the same. Ask students which version they would write in a story, and why.

Independent Work

Go to page 4 of the Notebook file. This gives the basic structure of a later scene in the Red Riding Hood story. Discuss where dialogue could be introduced in this scene (for example, between Grandma and the wolf, before and after he enters the cottage). Place a limit of three sentences of direct speech.

Wrap-Up

Listen to some students' scenes. Alternatively, write up interesting sentences. Discuss how characters are being presented. Point out that using direct speech gives greater impact to characters' words.

Writing for an Audience

Learning objective
- To adapt sentence construction to different readers.

Resources
- "Writing for an Audience" Notebook file
- individual whiteboards and pens
- writing materials

Whiteboard tools
- Pen tray
- Highlighter pen
- Select tool
- On-screen Keyboard

Getting Started

Ask: *What do you like reading? Why?* Focus on style, language, sentence construction, and tone, rather than subject. Ask: *What advice would you give for writing for your age group?* Compare ideas and agree on the top three rules. Write them on page 2 of the "Writing for an Audience" Notebook file, under the heading "Ages 9–12," for example:

- Use a variety of sentences.
- Don't make your sentences too long.
- Include complex sentences with interesting transitions.

Mini-Lesson

1. Go to page 3 of the Notebook file. Identify places where the writer has followed the golden rules decided by the class. Discuss other rules that the writer seems to have followed. Add them to the list on page 2, for example:
   - Give plenty of detail and description.
   - Use questions as well as statements.
   - Use interesting, informative vocabulary (*isolated*, *furtively*, *rattled*).
   - Involve the reader, making the reader feel you are talking directly to him or her.
2. Explain that writers write for different readers by varying their rules. On the right-hand column on page 2, work together to create a list of golden rules for writing for 5- to 6-year-olds, for example:
   a. Have pictures as well as text.
   b. Keep sentences short.
   c. Only have simple sentences.
   d. Use statements, not questions.
   e. Use easy, straightforward vocabulary.
3. Go to page 4 and read the story with students. Analyze the story, identifying where the writer has followed the rules.
4. Compare the picture story to the narrative on page 3. Discuss and mark up how the narrative has been broken up into six pages for the picture story.
5. Go to page 5 and read the text out loud. Ask: *Which of the two age groups is this for?* (9- to 12-year-olds) Highlight the details that show this.
6. Print a copy of page 5 for each pair of students. Display the golden rules on page 2.

Independent Work

Ask students to rewrite the story of Cinderella for a 5- to 6-year-old reader. Suggest retelling the story in six pages. Students must write text for each page and make notes on what the pictures will be.

Wrap-Up

Write a sentence plan for one of the students' stories on page 6 of the Notebook file. Scan and view more stories on screen, inviting students to talk about their planned pictures. (Upload scanned images by selecting Insert, then Picture File, and browsing to where you have saved the image.)

Note-taking

Learning objectives

- To identify and summarize evidence from a text.
- To use knowledge of different organizational features of texts to find information effectively.

Resources

- "Note-taking" Notebook file
- printed copy of page 3 of the Notebook file for each student
- paper and pens

Whiteboard tools

- Pen tray
- Highlighter pen
- Select tool
- On-screen Keyboard
- Delete button

Getting Started

Look at any charts of information displayed around the classroom. Ask: *Do you think these charts present information effectively? Which do you find easiest to understand? Why? How would you improve these charts?* Share and list ideas on page 2 of the "Note-taking" Notebook file. Ideas could include:

- less text
- more diagrams
- division of chart into sections
- headings
- numbers

Mini-Lesson

1. Read the text on page 3 of the Notebook file, explaining how plants make their food.
2. Focus on the three main paragraphs describing the process. Highlight the words that begin these paragraphs: *The first thing . . . This means that . . . After that . . .*
3. Explain that you want to make a chart about the process. Start by identifying the main information in each paragraph. Model how to summarize each paragraph. Highlight key words and phrases.
4. On page 4, type a sentence for each paragraph, each in its own separate text box. Agree on a title and type this in a separate text box, for example:

   How Plants Make Their Food

   - The plant absorbs water and air.
   - The plant gets energy from the sun.
   - The plant makes its food through photosynthesis.
5. Would students find this a helpful chart? Agree on the need for a better format. Suggest a flowchart format.
6. Delete the box on the left-hand side of the screen. The numbered parts of the flowchart represent the three steps in the process.
7. Move the phrases next to the correct part of the flowchart.
8. Discuss what else to add (for example, diagrams). Let students comment critically on the proposed chart.

Independent Work

Give each child a printout of page 3 of the Notebook file. Ask them to plan a diagram or chart using the printout. They should focus on the three main paragraphs highlighted earlier. Remind students to highlight key words before summarizing each of the three paragraphs in a short sentence or phrase. Their planning should include headings and diagrams. The charts can be completed in another session.

Wrap-Up

Scan and display students' flowcharts on page 5 of the Notebook file for discussion. (Upload scanned images by selecting Insert, then Picture File, and browsing to where you have saved the image.)

Instructional Texts

Learning objectives

- To compare information texts and identify how they are structured.
- To adapt sentence structure to different text-types, purposes, and readers.

Resources

- "Instructional Texts" Notebook file
- writing materials

(Microsoft Word is required to view the embedded text document in the Notebook file.)

Whiteboard tools

- Pen tray
- Select tool
- On-screen Keyboard
- Highlighter pen
- Page Sorter

Getting Started

Read the sentences on page 2 of the "Instructional Texts" Notebook file. Allow students time to think before prompting them to tell you about sentence types. Conclude that they are all imperative sentences. Ask: *How can you tell?* Guide students to notice the imperative verbs (*keep*, *watch*, *look*, *tell*). Give students practice in making up imperative sentences.

Mini-Lesson

1. Discuss the context for imperative sentences. Ask: *When/where do you read imperative sentences?* (In instructions) Talk about everyday examples, such as instructions in games or recipes.
2. Look around the classroom, checking for sets of instructions. Talk about notices around the school—for example, next to the fire extinguisher, near an alarm button, or in the computer room.
3. On page 3 of the Notebook file, make a list of features important to an instructional text.
4. Press on the star to show the ready-made list. Add any features that students have not identified by highlighting the text and dragging it onto page 3 in the Page Sorter.
5. Look at the text on page 4—a set of instructions to create a spelling poster display. Ask: *Where would you find this text?* (In a school textbook; on a worksheet)
6. Investigate the text more closely to identify and highlight imperative sentences.
7. Point out "The children can plan their collages and paintings on the computers." Ask: *What is wrong with this sentence?* (It is a statement.) Experiment with converting it to a command: "Plan the collages and paintings on the computers."
8. Experiment with including other features, such as bullet points.
9. Press on the button to edit the text as a Microsoft Word document. Stress the need for clarity. Page 5 demonstrates a possible result.

Independent Work

Return to the list of important features on page 3 of the Notebook file. Ask students to write a set of instructions to support practical work in the computer lab. For example, they could write a set of instructions to control a simple device (such as a buzzer, small motor, or lights) or to create a moving toy.

Support less-confident learners by allowing them to discuss their instructions with a partner first. As an extra challenge, ask more-confident learners to write a set of instructions on how to improve a classroom or school.

Wrap-Up

Use the scanner to upload students' instructions to page 6 of the Notebook file. (Upload scanned images by selecting Insert, then Picture File, and browsing to where you have saved the image.) Discuss clarity and usefulness. Provide opportunities for personal or partner evaluation as instructions are tested.

Summarizing

Learning objective

- To choose and combine words, images, and other features for particular effects.

Resources

- "Summarizing" Notebook file
- access to computers or a copy of page 12 of the Notebook file, one per student

(Microsoft Word is required to view the embedded text documents in the Notebook file.)

Whiteboard tools

- Eraser
- Pen tray
- Select tool
- Highlighter pen
- On-screen Keyboard

Getting Started

Open the "Summarizing" Notebook file and display page 2. Give students some oral instructions, making them deliberately long-winded. For example:

Look very closely and carefully at the SMART Board. Check absolutely before you go further that you can see properly. Take out just about all the materials you could possibly need for this lesson.

Ask students to comment on your language. (You used a lot of unnecessary words.) Encourage suggestions as to how these instructions could be given more briefly. Stress the need to retain important meanings.

Mini-Lesson

1. Go to page 3 of the Notebook file. Ask students to help you identify and highlight words that are key to meaning. Identify words that can be deleted, using a different highlighter color, until you have simpler sentences. Erase the blue marks to reveal the sample answers beneath each sentence.
2. Read the sentence on page 4. Identify and highlight the key words: *whiteboard; seen*. Discuss the message: *Whiteboards need to be in the right place to be viewed.*
3. Type suggestions to summarize the sentence in 12 words or less. For example:
   - *Whiteboards, put in a good spot, can be seen by all.*
   - *Whiteboards in a good spot can be seen by all.*
4. Investigate the shortened sentences. Identify the words that were left out. Point out where sentence construction has changed.
5. Suggest that new vocabulary can help with summarizing. Reveal the final sentence: *Well-positioned whiteboards give good visibility.* Point out that "good visibility" (two words) expresses the same meaning as "can be seen by all" (five words).
6. Go to page 5. Explain to students that you want to reduce the paragraph from 41 words to 20 words or less.
7. Work together to edit the text in the white box using the On-screen Keyboard. Focus on one sentence at a time, reminding students to think about key words and main messages—for example: *Titus agreed and disagreed. The camp would run out of special supplies if everyone ate them. What should he do?*

Independent Work

Go to page 6 of the Notebook file. Print out a copy of this text for every child or open the editable documents and make the text accessible on students' computers. The paragraph has 61 words. Ask students to reduce it to a summary of about 40 words.

Wrap-Up

Invite students to read their summaries out loud. Display students' edited documents on page 7 of the Notebook file. Stress the need to retain important elements.

Complex Sentences

Learning objectives
- To use different narrative techniques to engage and entertain the reader.
- To express subtle distinctions of meaning by constructing sentences in varied ways.

Resources
- "Complex Sentences" Notebook file
- writing notebooks and pens
- individual whiteboards and pens

Whiteboard tools
- Pen tray
- Select tool
- Fill Color tool
- Highlighter pen
- On-screen Keyboard

Getting Started

Open page 2 of the "Complex Sentences" Notebook file. Explain to students that you would like them to work on their individual whiteboards to punctuate the text so that there are four sentences. Ask them to number the sentences 1 to 4. Double-click on the text and type over to punctuate it, before pressing the red box to see the correct version. Ask: *Which three sentences belong together?* (Numbers 1, 2, and 3) *Why?* (They are complex sentences; sentence 4 is simple.) Use the Fill Color tool to fill the red panels with white to reveal the answers.

Mini-Lesson

1. Go to page 4 of the Notebook file. Ask students to explain the two sentence types. Pull the tabs to reveal the definitions.
2. Focus on the complex sentences from Getting Started. Investigate sentence 2. Ask: *Which is the main clause? How is the main clause joined to the subordinate clause?* Use a Highlighter pen to highlight the main clause (*Elephant trumpeted greetings*) and the conjunction (*until*).
3. Investigate complex sentences 1 and 3 on page 5. Highlight the words beginning the subordinate clauses. (*Sensing* and *Pleased*) Explain that these clauses are called *participial phrases*.
4. Look at the extra sentence on page 5. Ask: *Is this simple or complex? How are the clauses joined?* Pull the tabs to show that a semicolon can join clauses.
5. Move on to page 6 to begin the multiple-choice activity. Allow time for students to record their answer on individual whiteboards. Press the chosen answer to hear a sound effect, which indicates whether it is correct.
6. Continue the activity on pages 7 to 17. Encourage students to identify complex sentence features: main clauses, subordinate clauses, varied positions for conjunctions, commas, participial phrases.
7. Display page 18. Give students oral practice in creating simple and complex sentences. Encourage them to work with partners to identify effective complex sentences and simple sentences that can be linked to form complex sentences.
8. Point out that effective writing usually has a mixture of simple and complex sentences. Discuss the merits of both sentence types and annotate the appropriate boxes with students' ideas. Pull the tabs to reveal examples of the merits of each type of sentence.

Independent Work

Go to page 19 of the Notebook file. Ask students to write more about Tiger, using a mixture of simple and complex sentences. Emphasize varying the way clauses are linked in the complex sentences.

Wrap-Up

Choose one child to write some of their further sentences about Tiger on page 20 of the Notebook file. Encourage students to identify sentence types and links between clauses.

Connecting Ideas

Learning objectives

- To analyze the use of persuasive language.
- To adapt non-narrative forms and styles to write factual texts.
- To adapt sentence structure to different text-types, purposes, and readers.

Resources

- "Connecting Ideas" Notebook file
- a local traffic issue for discussion (for example, a proposed, possible, or recent change, such as a one-way street, bicycle lanes, speed ramps near school, or a pedestrian crossing)
- individual whiteboards and pens
- pens and paper

Whiteboard tools

- Pen tray
- Select tool
- On-screen Keyboard
- Highlighter pen

Getting Started

Introduce and outline the local traffic issue on page 2 of the "Connecting Ideas" Notebook file. Give out pens and paper. Working in pairs, have students consider both sides of the issue—one arguing for the change, the other against. Have them each write two or three points supporting their view, compare ideas, and take turns to argue their case. Ask: *Can you reach a conclusion?* Tell students that they will be learning how to connect their ideas to construct a balanced argument. They will need their notes later on in the lesson.

Mini-Lesson

1. Go to page 3 of the Notebook file. Type short sentences and link them with transition words. Highlight the transitions and explain that these can be used within sentences, between sentences, and between paragraphs, to link ideas. The transitions may be single words (*later*) or adverbial phrases (*later in the day*).
2. Go to page 4. Transitions can link cause and effect. Ask students to add a sentence to precede "I was late this morning because of this" (for example, "I missed the bus."). Ask: *What is the transition?* (because of this) *What type of information does it introduce?* (The effect of the first sentence)
3. Repeat with different sentences and the transition "as a consequence."
4. Read the text on page 5. Students should listen for and write down transitions linked to cause and effect and then show you the answers: *Therefore*; *Consequently*; *In consequence*; *As a result*.
5. Work together identifying and highlighting adverbial transitions in the text: *Therefore*; *On the one hand*; *In addition*; *Furthermore*; *On the other hand*; *Meanwhile*; *Conversely*; *Consequently*; *In addition*; *Nevertheless*; *In consequence*; *As a result*.
6. Read the third paragraph. Focus on this adverbial transition: *On the other hand*. Ask: *What does this transition link to?* (It introduces the other side, the counterargument to a point.) Ask students to identify other counterargument transitions in paragraphs 4 (*Conversely*) and 5 (*Nevertheless*).
7. Go to page 6. Discuss students' points from the Getting Started and note some on the SMART Board.

Independent Work

Have students write a newspaper article about a local traffic issue that includes points on both sides of the argument. Emphasize the need for transition links between sentences.

Wrap-Up

Invite students to share their work. Identify adverbial transitions and make a note of good examples of connecting ideas on page 7 of the Notebook file. Display page 8. Encourage students to vote on whether they agree or disagree with the issue.

Paragraphs

Learning objective
- To use paragraphs to achieve pace and emphasis.

Resources
- "Paragraphs" Notebook file
- "Penguins" (p. 68)
- individual whiteboards and pens

Whiteboard tools
- Eraser
- Pen tray
- Highlighter pen
- Select tool
- On-screen Keyboard
- Delete button

Getting Started

Display page 2 of the "Paragraphs" Notebook file. Tell students that they have three minutes to make notes for one paragraph, recounting what the class did during a recent school event. Ask them to decide how many sentences they would need and, using numbers and letters, to identify which notes they would use for which sentence. Have students compare results with a partner, discussing sentence order. Add some examples to the Notebook file.

Mini-Lesson

1. Move on to page 3 of the Notebook file. Review the term *paragraph*. Ask students for suggested definitions of the word before pulling the tab to reveal a definition: a group of sentences that fit together well.
2. Read the piece of text on Jackie Robinson on page 4. Discuss the structure of this paragraph and the order in which information is presented.
3. Go to page 5 for some facts about frogs. Explain that these can be notes for one paragraph of an expository report that students are going to write on frogs.
4. Remove the yellow box to reveal a first attempt at writing the paragraph (Version 1). Do students think the information is in the best possible order? Agree on a better order, annotating the text or moving the sentences around.
5. Reveal the second draft (Version 2) on page 6. Ask students to read and discuss it with a partner, then write a critical comment on their individual whiteboards. Compare comments and add a selection to the Notebook page. Agree on certain weaknesses, such as dull sentences and sentences that are not connected to one another.
6. Work together orally, annotating the text on the SMART Board with students' suggestions before revealing the final version (Version 3) on page 7. Ask: *How has this version been improved?* Remove the yellow box to point out improvements made by the addition of details (for example, words such as *powerful*, *quickly*) and transition words used to create links within the paragraph (for example: *Because of*; *This*; *As a result*). Emphasize the improved structure of this paragraph.

Independent Work

Ask students to construct a paragraph about penguins. The facts that will provide the basis are on page 8 of the Notebook file. Provide each child with a copy of "Penguins" (p. 68). A first draft has already been provided. Students should write:

- Version 2: with improved sentence order
- Version 3: with added detail, improved structure, and transitions

Wrap-Up

Write or type some of the paragraphs on page 9 of the Notebook file. Highlight and discuss good examples of added details and transitions in Version 3.

Connecting Paragraphs

Learning objectives

- To use varied structures to shape and organize text coherently.
- To use paragraphs to achieve pace and emphasis.

Resources

- "Connecting Paragraphs" Notebook file
- "Paragraph Planning" (p. 69)
- individual whiteboards and pens

Whiteboard tools

- Pen tray
- Highlighter pen
- Select tool
- Delete button
- On-screen Keyboard

Getting Started

Go to page 2 of the "Connecting Paragraphs" Notebook file. Allow three minutes for students to write notes about school yesterday on their individual whiteboards. Use the interactive timer to time them. Ask them to decide how many paragraphs they would use if they were writing the notes into a narrative. Then ask them to decide which notes they would need for which paragraph, using numbers and letters. Have students compare results with a partner.

Mini-Lesson

1. Look at the text about Jackie Robinson on page 3 of the Notebook file. Ask students to read the text and to write a single-word label on their whiteboards for the contents of each paragraph.
2. Compare results and annotate the SMART Board with students' suggestions.
3. Go to page 4. Invite students to look at a piece of their own writing (for example, a science explanation). Ask them to choose one paragraph from the middle, and to write down why they began that new paragraph at a certain point.
4. Compare answers, discussing how they linked the paragraph to the rest of the text. Write or type some examples on the page.
5. Point out that decisions about starting a new paragraph are not easy; the progress of a text is not always linear (for example, the second paragraph on page 3 moves sideways, rather than forward, chronologically as it expands on the basic information in the first paragraph).
6. Look at the text on pages 5 and 6, "Online Progress." Invite students to read the text with a partner and to think of a single-word label for the content of each paragraph. Share ideas, annotating the text. Move the yellow panels to reveal some examples.
7. Ask: *Does the narrative progress chronologically?* Point out how it begins on Monday morning, but moves back in time to explain changes in Henry.
8. Encourage students to identify the transition words that start each paragraph. Highlight these in the text and discuss how they help the reader make sense of the narrative.

Independent Work

Go to page 7 of the Notebook file. Ask students to plan paragraphs for the next part of this story using "Paragraph Planning" (p. 69). First, they should give the paragraphs single-word labels. Then, they should write notes about what will occur in the paragraph and how it will fit in with the rest of the story. For Stage 3, students need to provide the opening for each paragraph as well as the transition words.

Wrap-Up

Write or type some students' ideas in the table on page 8 of the Noteboook file. Save these for a future lesson.

Writing Narratives

Learning objectives

- To understand how writers use different structures to create coherence and impact.
- To use different narrative techniques to engage and entertain the reader.
- To use varied structures to shape and organize text coherently.

Resources

- "Writing Narratives" Notebook file
- independent work from "Connecting Paragraphs" (p. 32)
- individual whiteboards and pens
- writing materials

Whiteboard tools

- Pen tray
- Highlighter pen
- Select tool
- On-screen Keyboard

Getting Started

Go to page 2 of the "Writing Narratives" Notebook file which shows paragraph 5 of the story "Online Progress" from the "Connecting Paragraphs" lesson (p. 32). Ask students to note, on their individual whiteboards, what they think should be noticed in this paragraph, and why.

Mini-Lesson

1. Share ideas about how you might annotate the text on-screen, for example:

WORDS	ANNOTATION
This morning	The time transition links the paragraph to previous ones and signals a return to the immediate present of paragraph 1.
Jim	A new character is introduced. The reader knows that he is Henry's father, referred to at the end of the previous paragraph.
at home	There is a change of setting.
Prime numbers, weather patterns, insulators, and bipeds	The writer emphasizes the extent of the work to cover.
Tumbled	This is an effective verb, giving a strong visual picture of questions landing quickly on the computer screen.
Nevertheless	This transition structures and links sentences within the paragraph.
Thumbing	The word conveys a clear visual picture of Jim, in an old-fashioned way, turning pages of books, hinting that Jim is happier using books than computers. (The writer hints rather than telling the reader directly.)
Unfortunately	This transition within the paragraph signals that something bad will occur.
Hurtling	This word reinforces the earlier images of a lot of work arriving quickly.
Computer	Ending the paragraph suggests that a change is coming.
Suddenly	This transition injects drama and suspense into the story. Could this be a place to end the chapter?

2. Talk about what could happen in the story. (Remind students about the plans they made in "Connecting Paragraphs.")
3. Use page 3 to review the important writing techniques. Press the button to view a list of some of the techniques used.

Independent Work

Display page 4 of the Notebook file. Ask students to read (amending as they wish) their story plans. Invite them to write the next section of the story.

Wrap-Up

Invite students to type or write some paragraph examples on page 5 of the Notebook file. Point out examples of effective writing techniques.

Persuasive Ads

Learning objective
- To recognize rhetorical devices used to argue, persuade, mislead, and sway the reader.

Resources
- "Persuasive Ads" Notebook file
- individual whiteboards and pens
- computers (optional)
- writing materials

Whiteboard tools
- Eraser
- Pen tray
- Select tool
- Highlighter pen
- On-screen Keyboard

Getting Started

Display page 2 of the "Persuasive Ads" Notebook file. Ask students to write three advertising slogans they can remember on their individual whiteboards. Invite them to compare results with a partner. Ask: *How can you remember those slogans?* Compare the class results. Identify a slogan chosen by a number of students and discuss why it is memorable.

Mini-Lesson

1. Show page 3 of the Notebook file, which features a picture of a cell phone. Ask: *What type of text do you think should go with this picture?* Remove the blue panel to reveal the answer. (Persuasive)
2. Allow partner discussion as students share ideas for what the text should say. Suggest questions to consider, such as: *What is the text's purpose? Who is the audience?*
3. Encourage students to make notes of their ideas on their individual whiteboards.
4. Discuss ideas as a class, adding suggestions to the Notebook page.
5. Reveal the completed advertisement on page 4. Encourage analysis using the questions written beside the advertisement, annotating students' responses.
6. Go to page 5. Explain that these are stages in an advertisement's planning:
   a. Purpose and audience
   b. Word level
   c. Sentence level
   d. Text level
7. Discuss each stage, writing in the boxes as you agree on important questions to consider at that stage.
8. Delete the shapes to reveal some examples.
9. Return to this page when students are completing their independent work.

Independent Work

Display page 6 of the Notebook file. Tell students that they are going to plan a magazine advertisement for a healthy food product. Explain that the advertisement will be aimed at young people. Encourage students to use either paper or computers for initial drafts.

Support less-confident learners with a choice of products. As an extra challenge, ask more-confident learners to advertise the same product for a different audience.

Wrap-Up

Ask students to share their advertisements in small groups. Encourage them to read and evaluate one another's work. Draw particular attention to effective word-level techniques. Write or type good examples on page 7 of the Notebook file.

Writing Poetry

Learning objective

- To choose and combine words, images, and other features for particular effects.

Resources

- "Writing Poetry" Notebook file
- "A Seaside Trip" (p. 70)
- individual whiteboards and pens

Whiteboard tools

- Pen tray
- Select tool
- On-screen Keyboard
- Page Sorter

Getting Started

Read the poem "A Seaside Trip" (p. 70) to students. (Do not display the words.) Discuss what the poem is about and what made it enjoyable to listen to. (Length of lines, rhythm, vocabulary) Read the poem again. Ask students to write on individual whiteboards the words or phrases that stick in their mind. Compare results, writing popular words and phrases on page 2 of the "Writing Poetry" Notebook file. Suggest that for a poem to be successful when read aloud, it needs to contain evocative and memorable words and phrases.

Mini-Lesson

1. Open page 3 of the Notebook file. Discuss what is meant by *themes*.
2. Investigate the text. Identify and circle evocative words that convey the first theme (for example, *speeding*, *fleeting glimpses*, *plunged*). Separate these words from the rest of the text and drag them into the appropriate box.
3. Repeat the process for the second theme (for example, *the twisting line*; *unfamiliar countryside*) and the third theme (for example, *sinister dream*; *threatening landscape*; *twisted trees*; *menacing branches*).
4. Now copy the individual words onto page 4. Explain that you want students to write a performance poem (a poem that is written to be read aloud). Press the box at the bottom of the page to read the important features of a performance poem. Add more features if students have any further ideas about performance poems.
5. Discuss how to achieve these aims in a performance poem about the strange train journey. Ideas could include: a quick rhythm (to match the train); short, jerky lines; evocative words.
6. Suggest that the words and phrases taken from the passage could form the basis of a performance poem. Move these words to the edges of the screen, leaving the central area free.
7. With students' input, use the central area to write sample lines. Introduce new vocabulary, in addition to dragging words from the edges of the screen into your lines of poetry.
8. Start to build up a poem with the class. Demonstrate making revisions: delete and substitute words, reorganize words and lines, and experiment with figurative language.

Independent Work

Ask students to write a performance poem about the train journey, using some of the words chosen from the narrative. Encourage revision of rough drafts before producing a polished poem. Less-confident learners could work with a partner.

Wrap-Up

Invite students to perform their poems. Which words and phrases do listeners remember? Write good examples on page 5 of the Notebook file.

Imagery

Learning objective
- To infer writers' perspectives from what is written and from what is implied.

Resources
- "Imagery" Notebook file
- writing materials

Whiteboard tools
- Pen tray
- Select tool
- Highlighter pen

Getting Started

Go to page 2 of the "Imagery" Notebook file and ask students to look around the classroom: at the room, the people in it, and what is happening. Ask: *What descriptive word comes into your mind?* Note students' responses. Start combining and adding to words to create some descriptive lines of poetry or prose. Ask students to shut their eyes as you read lines aloud. Ask: *How vivid are the visual images?*

Mini-Lesson

1. Go to page 3 of the Notebook file. Tell students that these poems have been written in the same way as in the Getting Started activity. Point out that both poems are called "Our Classroom." Read them aloud.
2. Ask students to identify words that may have been starting points: *wintry, steamy, noisy, rushing, busy, lunch*. Highlight them.
3. Ask: *How do the poems differ in their language?* (The first poem describes the classroom in straightforward language; the second poem describes the classroom as a kitchen.)
4. Define *literal language* and *figurative language*. Ask students to vote on which poem uses which type of language. (Poem (a) uses literal language: words are used with their normal meanings. Poem (b) uses figurative language: words do not have their usual meanings.)
5. Investigate poem (b). Ask: *Who is the rushing, harassed cook?* (The teacher) *What is the meal?* (The lesson) *What is the gong?* (The bell)
6. Point out that the metaphor of the classroom as a kitchen is carried throughout the poem. The figurative language creates a strong visual image.
7. Look at the picture on page 4. Discuss when and where the scene is set. (An old-fashioned schoolroom, probably from pioneer days) Working in pairs, give students time to think of and suggest words to describe the room, atmosphere, people, or feelings shown. Annotate the picture with students' suggestions.
8. Suggest that some of these words could be the starting point for a poem or descriptive passage about the lesson shown in the photograph.

Independent Work

Ask students to write their poetry or prose about the classroom scene, making initial rough drafts. Encourage them to use figurative language to bring the picture to life.

Less-confident learners could be given starting lines and be allowed to work in pairs. As an extra challenge, ask more-confident learners to write a poem or prose passage about their school.

Wrap-Up

Invite students to read their work to the rest of the class. Display the image on page 4 of the Notebook file. How well do the words match the scene? Pages 5 and 6 offer an opportunity to assess students' understanding of literal and figurative language.

Similes, Metaphors & Personification

Learning objectives
- To select words and language, drawing on knowledge of literary features.
- To integrate words, images, and sounds imaginatively for different purposes.

Resources
- "Similes, Metaphors & Personification" Notebook file
- individual whiteboards and pens
- notebooks and pens
- computers with word-processing application (if available)

Whiteboard tools
- Eraser
- Pen tray
- Select tool
- Delete button
- On-screen Keyboard

Getting Started

Pair up students and ask them to explain the terms *simile* and *metaphor* to each other. Have them write an example of each. Go to page 2 of the "Similes, Metaphors & Personification" Notebook file, which shows a table divided into similes and metaphors. Have students decide on which side of the table their examples belong.

Mini-Lesson

1. Go to page 3 of the Notebook file. Explain that similes and metaphors are devices for creating a strong image in the reader's mind. They are particularly effective in poems. Ask students to define the terms *simile* and *metaphor* before deleting or moving the panels to reveal the definitions.
2. Return to page 2 and ask: *Are any sentences in the wrong section?* Erase and rewrite as necessary.
3. Display page 4 to remind students of the purpose of a simile—to create a strong visual image. In order to do this, the comparison must be unusual but still have an obvious link to the subject. Use the Eraser from the Pen tray to reveal examples.
4. Move on to page 5 and make a list of classroom objects. Work together to create a few similes, reminding students of their purpose as outlined on page 4.
5. Tell students that they are going to turn the similes they created into metaphors, writing their ideas on their individual whiteboards. Go to page 6 and reveal the example behind the panel. Write some of students' ideas in the space provided.
6. On page 7, focus on the example about the clock. Point out that the image makes the clock into a person. It is therefore a metaphor, but also an example of *personification.* Ask: *What does personification mean?* Delete the panel to reveal a definition and an example. Point out that personification lets the poet extend a metaphor beyond the initial image.
7. Ask students to extend the metaphor on page 8. Let them experiment on their whiteboards before revealing the example behind the panel.
8. Press the button to return to students' examples of metaphors on page 6. Challenge them to extend these in the same way.

Independent Work

Go to page 9 of the Notebook file and ask students to write a poem about "The Living Classroom," using personification of the classroom's objects. Encourage students to make some initial rough drafts. They could use a word-processing application, if computers are available, to make it easier for them to edit and improve their work.

Wrap-Up

Invite individuals to read their poems aloud, and ask the audience about the images that form in their minds. Write or type some of students' suggestions on page 10 of the Notebook file.

Idioms

Learning objective
- To explore how word meanings change when used in different contexts.

Resources
- "Idioms" Notebook file
- individual whiteboards and pens
- writing materials

Whiteboard tools
- Eraser
- Pen tray
- Select tool
- On-screen Keyboard
- Delete button

Getting Started

Go to page 2 of the "Idioms" Notebook file and ask students to make a sentence from each line of words on their individual whiteboards (they must use all the words). Compare results.

Drag to rearrange the words on the SMART Board. Ask: *What are the sentences called?* Pull the tab to identify the sentences as *idioms*.

Mini-Lesson

1. Read the heading on page 3 of the Notebook file. Can students tell you what an idiom is? Listen to their suggestions before deleting the panel to reveal the answer: *A short saying in general use. An idiom has origins in the past and may have changed a little over time; it states a belief about the world.*
2. Look at the beginnings of the idioms on the page and ask students if they can complete them. Use the Eraser to reveal the answers.
3. Move on to page 4. Investigate the literal meanings of these two idioms. Delete the panels to reveal examples. Ask: *What pictures would you use to illustrate these idioms?*
4. Go to page 5. Give students time to work out with their partner what these idioms might mean in modern, general language. Remove the panels to reveal some examples.
5. Ask students to think of situations when they could say or write these idioms. Share ideas before revealing the examples at the bottom of the page.
6. Look at the pictures and idioms on page 6. Ask students to figure out which idiom fits which picture. They should write matching letters and numbers on individual whiteboards (such as 1–e). Move the idioms to their matching picture or remove the green box to reveal the answers.
7. Using page 7, explain that pictures have now been replaced by modern word descriptions. Repeat the task of matching letters and numbers. Move the idioms to their corresponding situation and remove the box to reveal the answers.

Independent Work

Go to page 8 of the Notebook file. Ask students to use their whiteboards, or paper, to draw two boxes for each idiom—one box should illustrate the idiom's literal meaning; the other box should describe briefly, in words, modern situations to suit it.

Support less-confident learners with picture suggestions. As an extra challenge, encourage more-confident learners to find other idioms.

Wrap-Up

Invite the children to share their answers. Write or type some examples on page 9. Address any misconceptions about meanings.

Reading Journals

Learning objective
- To reflect on reading habits and preferences.

Resources
- "Reading Journals" Notebook file
- "Reading Journal Entry" (p. 71)

Whiteboard tools
- Pen tray
- On-screen Keyboard
- Select tool
- Highlighter pen

Getting Started

Open page 2 of the "Reading Journals" Notebook file. Working in pairs, have students take turns "selling" a favorite book to their partner. Afterward, ask: *What did the speakers need to say?* (Enough to make the book seem worth reading) *What did the listeners want to hear?* (Not so much that there was no point in reading the book) Make notes on page 2 and suggest that book reviews need to do this, too. Repeat the "selling" exercise, taking into account these points.

Mini-Lesson

1. Read a book review to the class. Ask: *When is the best time to write a book review?* (When you finish the book) *Why might this be a problem?* (You might forget early reactions or predictions.)
2. Point out the advantage of keeping a reading journal. Used regularly, it could show how you feel at different stages of the book.
3. Discuss information that could be useful in a reading journal entry. Make a list on page 3 of the Notebook file. For example:
   - title
   - author
   - first impressions
   - cover
   - story opening
   - predictions
   - changes in opinion
   - memorable incidents or words
   - thoughts on how the story will finish
   - recommendations
4. Read the story on page 4. The story is written for younger children. It is short, so would probably need only one reading journal entry.
5. Read the completed journal entry for this picture story on page 5. Point out important features, such as:
   - mention of the cover
   - references to memorable details in the pictures
   - quoting of words from the text
   - recommendation about who might enjoy the book

Independent Work

Display the story opening on page 6 of the Notebook file. Give out copies of "Reading Journal Entry" (p. 71). Ask students to read the story opening and then write a journal entry. Remind them to make a prediction about the rest of the book.

Wrap-Up

Insert scanned examples of students' journal pages onto page 7 of the Notebook file, or discuss and write up their ideas. Talk about students' different reactions to the story and their predictions. Did the story opening entice them to read further? Encourage students to start keeping a journal, using the layout on the reproducible sheet or designing their own layout.

Making Notes

Learning objective
- To make notes on and use evidence from across a text to explain events or ideas.

Resources
- "Making Notes" Notebook file
- printouts of pages 4 and 5 of the Notebook file, one for each student
- copy of page 7 of the Notebook file
- prepared Notebook page of your own notes based on this information

Whiteboard tools
- Pen tray
- Highlighter pen
- Select tool
- Page Sorter

Getting Started

Read aloud the scurvy passage from page 7 of the "Making Notes" Notebook file, without letting students see the text (press the red box at the bottom of page 2 to jump to page 7). Ask them to write quick notes on their individual whiteboards. Share the notes, and list on page 2 the key information that they all identified.

Mini-Lesson

1. Explain that notes should be short and quick to write, using words and phrases, not sentences. Go to page 3 of the Notebook file and discuss the list of important features of notes.
2. Refer to the last point in the list. Point out that students wrote notes for themselves in the Getting Started activity.
3. Show students your own notes on the passage. Ask: *What would you do differently?* Demonstrate any changes they suggest.
4. Ask students to compare their Getting Started notes with a partner's. Ask: *Does your partner understand your notes?*
5. Go to page 7, allowing students to compare this with their notes and with yours. Explain your thought process as you went over the passage, identifying essential information and words. Show how you used your own words (unless deliberately copying names or technical vocabulary).
6. Discuss possible problems when writing notes for other users. Remind students that notes must be written with the user in mind.

Independent Work

Ask students to read the report "Modern Eating" on pages 4 and 5 of the Notebook file. Give a printout of the two pages to each child. Ask them to write two sets of notes:

1. personal notes for their own use
2. notes suitable for someone else

Provide a list of essential and technical vocabulary for less-confident learners. Ask more-confident learners to make notes on another report.

Wrap-Up

Use the scanner to upload students' notes. (Upload scanned images by selecting Insert, then Picture file, and browsing to where you have saved the image.) Investigate the changes made between the first and second sets of notes. Make a note of these differences on page 6 of the Notebook file.

Point of View

Learning objective

- To compare the usefulness of techniques such as visualization and point of view in exploring the meaning of texts.

Resources

- "Point of View" Notebook file
- individual whiteboards and pens
- writing notebooks or paper and pens

Whiteboard tools

- Pen tray
- Select tool
- On-screen Keyboard
- Highlighter pen

Getting Started

Discuss the main events of the story "Cinderella" and list them on page 2 of the "Point of View" Notebook file. (Press on the red box to see an example list on page 9.) Ask: *Which character(s) do you feel sympathy for? Why?*

Mini-Lesson

1. Go to page 3 of the Notebook file. Choose one incident from "Cinderella" (for example, the day after the ball). Write up the facts: palace courtier arrives with the slipper; stepmother and two sisters try it on; Cinderella kept out of way; finally sent for.
2. Introduce and define the word *empathy*—the ability to identify with someone else. Most readers empathize with Cinderella, so they are likely to see things from her point of view. If parts of the story were told from another point of view, readers might empathize with a different character.
3. Demonstrate how the stepmother would tell the story: *In my opinion, Cinderella should be grateful for . . . From my point of view, she is lucky . . .* Point out the use of persuasive phrases (*in my opinion; from my point of view*) and their appropriate prepositions.
4. Divide the class into groups of four. Have each member take on the role of a different character and, in one to two minutes, retell part of the story from his or her own point of view, ensuring that the facts are correct, but trying to gain sympathy for him- or herself.
5. Move among the groups, making oral contributions. Afterward invite the class to listen to good examples. Discuss how and why these characters persuaded listeners to empathize with them (vocabulary; emphasis on one aspect of the situation; insight into feelings).
6. Read the text on page 4. Investigate how the nursery maid gains audience empathy by mentioning: how long she has waited for one day off (four weeks); the length of the walk home; vocabulary (*whole, first*); her feelings (excitement and then disappointment).

Independent Work

Ask students to write about the same incident from another character's point of view (for example, Nanny or the Mistress). They should retain facts, but emphasize new details, additional information, or a different perspective.

Wrap-Up

Scan some of the accounts and add them to page 5 of the Notebook file. (Upload scanned images by selecting Insert, then Picture File, and then browsing to where you have saved the image.) Ask the writers to perform them. Ask listeners: *How much empathy do you have for the character? Which words affect you?* Annotate and highlight words on the Notebook file. Go to page 6. Ask a volunteer to read the speech bubble. How far do students agree with Cinderella's point of view? Can they give reasons for their choices? Hold a class vote to give Cinderella an "empathy" rating.

Myths

Learning objectives
- To compare different types of narrative texts and identify how they are structured.
- To infer writers' perspectives from what is written and from what is implied.

Resources
- "Myths" Notebook file
- writing notebooks or paper and pens

Whiteboard tools
- Pen tray
- Select tool
- On-screen Keyboard

Getting Started

Read the story on pages 2 to 5 of the "Myths" Notebook file. Go to page 6 and ask: *Is this story fiction or nonfiction?* (Fiction) *Why?* (It is a story, not fact.) Make a note of students' responses.

Mini-Lesson

1. Ask: *What genre of story is "Pandora's Box"?* (Myth) Write this on page 6 of the Notebook file and discuss its meaning. Find a definition in an online encyclopedia.
2. Go to page 7. Ask: *What features do you expect in a myth?* Write a list, going back and highlighting relevant text in "Pandora's Box."
3. Pull out features of myths from the box on page 7.
4. Go to page 8 and ask: *Who was Zeus?* (The highest god in Greek mythology) Usc a Web site to find names of other Greek gods and goddesses. There are many more myths that involve different Greek gods.
5. Read the story again, asking students to think about the characters.
6. Go to page 9. Place an adjective inside the discussion circle (for example: *sensible*).
7. Ask a student to choose and place the appropriate character to join this word and to justify the choice—for example, *"Sensible describes Epimatheus because he left the box alone."*
8. Invite another student to make a change—person, adjective, or both—and explain his or her choice. Encourage reference to the text.
9. Vary the use of the discussion circle, for example, both characters could be inside with the same adjective(s) applicable.
10. Explain that our opinions of the characters have been molded by the writer's approach. The writer could have told the story differently, yet still kept the same facts. If Pandora was the narrator, she might have emphasized the importance of knowing the contents of the box.

Independent Work

Display or print page 10 of the Notebook file. Ask students to read the text on the page, and then rewrite it in their own words. They should retain facts, but treat Pandora sympathetically. They can write as the author, or let Pandora narrate.

Provide less-confident learners with a list of useful adjectives. Challenge more-confident learners to do the same with the third part of the story (see page 4 of the Notebook file).

Wrap-Up

Invite students to read their new versions of the second part of the story. Ensure that they can distinguish between an author's and a narrator's voice. Discuss new reactions to Pandora. Note down students' responses on page 11 of the Notebook file.

Fables

Learning objectives
- To tell a story using notes.
- To compare different types of narrative texts and identify how they are structured.
- To infer writers' perspectives from what is written and from what is implied.

Resources
- "Fables" Notebook file
- writing materials

Whiteboard tools
- Pen tray
- On-screen Keyboard
- Highlighter pen
- Select tool
- Page Sorter
- Fill Color tool

Getting Started

Open page 2 of the "Fables" Notebook file. Tell the fable "The Tortoise and the Hare." Use effective intonation, dramatic pauses, and voice changes to suit how or what is said. As you say the six cue words on the Notebook page, move them into the box. Point out how the cue words remind you of the key incidents. Ask: *How is listening to a story different from reading it?* (Intonation and pauses help you understand what is happening.)

Mini-Lesson

1. Read page 3 of the Notebook file and ask: *What does this story have in common with the Getting Started story?* (They are both fables.) Fables began as oral stories and many are attributed to Aesop, a Greek storyteller. Centuries later, these oral stories were put into writing.
2. Ask: *What helps you understand this written story?* (Written words and punctuation)
3. Highlight where punctuation guides the reader: for example, quotation marks and exclamation marks.
4. Ask: *What does this story teach us?* Press the button to reveal the moral.
5. Discuss the list of features of fables on page 4, identifying examples in the story on page 3.
6. Go to page 5. Discuss the moral of the story on page 3. Reveal one feature of a moral at a time (by using the Fill Color tool to fill each box with a light color) and discuss each feature in turn.
7. Return to page 2 and experiment with writing a moral for "The Tortoise and the Hare."
8. Go to page 6 and read the moral. Discuss ideas for an appropriate fable to go with it. Ask: *What animals would you use? What plot?* Add students' suggestions for animals and plots to the Notebook page.
9. Press the button to view some story suggestions. These can be selected and dragged to page 6 in the Page Sorter.

Independent Work

Have students create a pictorial storyboard of their fable, to act as a prompt for oral storytelling.

Allow less-confident learners to work in pairs. As an extra challenge, encourage more-confident learners to repeat the task with a new moral.

Wrap-Up

Add the scanned storyboards to page 7 of the Notebook file. (Upload scanned images by selecting Insert, then Picture File, and browsing to where you have saved the image.) Allow students to talk the class through their storyboards. Hold a storytelling session, with students using their storyboards for their cues.

Poetry & Words

Learning objectives
- To recognize how poets manipulate words.
- To investigate humorous verse.

Resources
- "Poetry and Words" Notebook file
- "Poem Interpretation" (p. 72)
- individual whiteboards and pens

Whiteboard tools
- Pen tray
- Select tool
- On-screen Keyboard
- Delete button

Getting Started

Go to page 2 of the "Poetry and Words" Notebook file. Ask students: *What is a homophone*? (A word with the same pronunciation, but different meaning and spelling, as another word) As a class, think of homophones for each of the words on the page. (For example: *paws* and *pause*; *stare* and *stair*) Ask students to write sentences using the words. Encourage them to think of sentences where the listener may think of both words. Listen to the sentences together and ask: *Can you always tell which word is being used?*

Mini-Lesson

1. Display page 3 of the Notebook file and tell students that you will be reading "Jabberwocky" by Lewis Carroll (pages 4 and 5). Ask students to identify and write, on individual whiteboards, the nonsense words they hear.
2. Invite them to write a definition for each word and then compare meanings with a partner. Write or type examples on page 6.
3. Remove the panel to suggest that all the meanings are correct. Discuss this together before revealing the answer beneath the rectangle at the bottom of the page. (The poet has used the sound and rhythm of the word to convey a mood but has left the audience free to make its own interpretation of the meaning.)
4. Go to page 7. Encourage students to read the title, "Daze of the Weak," and write on their individual whiteboards a comment on what the poem could be about. Share ideas. Did students notice the play on words?
5. Suggest that they close their eyes as you say the title. Ask: *How would you expect to spell the main words? Why?*
6. Reveal the first verse and ask students to read it. Ask: *Do you like it?* Allow time for partner discussion before you ask students to justify their answers. Encourage them to tell you whether they found the poem serious or humorous. Why or why not?
7. Ask students to identify examples of similar word play. Point out that sliding down a flume is usually associated with a water park, not sliding on a wet floor. Ask: *What is the double meaning of "Hit on"?* (Fell and realized) *Which one did you think of first?*

Independent Work

Remove the green rectangle to show the second verse on page 7 of the Notebook file and ask students to read it. Encourage them to think about, analyze, and interpret the words. Invite them to write about the verse, referring to the words.

Wrap-Up

Hold a class discussion on the second verse, "Wednesday." Encourage students to express their views. Write or type any key thoughts on page 8 of the Notebook file.

Reading Narratives

Learning objective
- To understand how writers use different structures to create coherence and impact.

Resources
- "Reading Narratives" Notebook file
- individual whiteboards and pens
- writing materials

Whiteboard tools
- Pen tray
- Highlighter pen
- Select tool
- Delete button

Getting Started

Go to page 2 of the "Reading Narratives" Notebook file. On their individual whiteboards, ask students to write down the titles of three adventure stories or novels. Ask students to hold up their whiteboards and look around. Check whether any titles appear on more than one whiteboard and discuss what is special about those books.

Mini-Lesson

1. Display page 3 of the Notebook file. Ask students to write what they feel the purpose of adventure fiction is. Compare their ideas before deleting the panels to reveal two suggestions: a) to entertain the reader; b) to remove the reader from everyday life.
2. Ask: *How does the writer achieve these aims?* Most students will focus on plot, but point out the additional importance of story structure, plus language and sentence construction.
3. Move on to page 4. Discuss the structure of an adventure book, annotating the page accordingly. Adventure novels consist of a build-up of events and complications. Ask: *When does the writer often finish a chapter?* (At a cliffhanger, when the reader wonders if danger or problems will be resolved)
4. Now discuss language and sentence construction. Explain that the writer's language and sentence construction may slip by unnoticed. Emphasize that to become effective writers, we need to know the techniques used.
5. Establish that the paragraph on page 5 is an excerpt from an adventure story. Identify writing techniques by making a close analysis of the language and sentences used. Draw attention to words by circling, highlighting, or numbering them.
6. With students' help, make annotations in the margin on the SMART Board page. Example annotations could be:

WORDS	ANNOTATION
Monday morning	Setting of time and place is established immediately.
Mr Davies; the class	The story is written in the third person.
Mr Davies; Henry	Characters are introduced quickly.
followed; tumbled	Verbs are in the past tense, usual in narratives.
Skeptical	This adjective highlights a difference of opinion from his colleagues.

Independent Work

Provide students with printed copies of page 6, which shows the next three paragraphs of the story. Invite them to read a paragraph, analyzing the text, before selecting points to draw attention to. Suggest numbering points and then ask students to make annotations, with corresponding numbers, on a separate piece of paper.

Wrap-Up

Work together on paragraph 2 of the excerpt. Listen to students' suggestions, using some to annotate the paragraph on page 7.

Nonfiction Texts

Learning objectives

- To review the conventions and features of different types of text.
- To review a range of nonfiction text types, discussing when a writer might choose to write in a given style and form.

Resources

- "Nonfiction Texts" Notebook file
- "Identify the Text Type" (p. 73)
- individual whiteboards and pens
- writing materials

Whiteboard tools

- Eraser
- Pen tray
- Highlighter pen
- Select tool
- On-screen Keyboard

Getting Started

Open the "Nonfiction Texts" Notebook file and go to page 2. On their individual whiteboards, ask students to write what they know about nonfiction texts. Encourage them to look in their science or social studies notebooks to identify the different types of writing they have done. Invite partners to compare findings. Write or type any examples on the Notebook page.

Mini-Lesson

1. Draw students' attention to the words in boxes on page 3 of the Notebook file: *recount*, *description*, and *instructions*. Ask students to consider what these text types have in common. (They are all nonfiction text types.)
2. Remind students that the text types have particular writing features. Consider the text types one at a time, asking students about important features. Write about five bullet points on each text type in the boxes. Pull the tabs to reveal examples, if required.
3. Move on to page 4, which shows the words *explanation*, *persuasion*, and *discussion*. Continue as before, making bulleted notes on these text types and revealing the examples if necessary.
4. Discuss and compare them to students' suggestions.
5. Point out that selection of text type, and therefore appropriate writing style, involves two factors: the writing's purpose and its audience.
6. Press the image on page 5 to open the "What type of text?" quiz. There are six multiple-choice questions in which students must select a text type for each purpose and audience.

Independent Work

Display page 6 of the Notebook file. Ask students to read the text excerpts on "Identify the Text Type" (p. 73). Invite them to draw arrows from the text type labels to each text. Ask students to write, on a separate piece of paper, the reasons for their choices.

Support less-confident learners with partner work. As an extra challenge, encourage more-confident learners to describe an audience and purpose for each text.

Wrap-Up

Go to page 7 of the Notebook file, which contains some of the text excerpts from the reproducible sheet. Take a vote to investigate students' choices. Ask students to write their answer on their individual whiteboards and take a tally of their votes. Annotate the texts and discuss reasons for their choices.

Book Review

Learning objectives

- To appraise a text quickly, deciding on its value, quality, or usefulness.
- To discuss personal reading with others.

Resources

- "Book Review" Notebook file
- individual whiteboards and pens
- writing materials
- a selection of chapter books

Whiteboard tools

- Pen tray
- Highlighter pen
- Pen tool
- On-screen Keyboard

Getting Started

Open the "Book Review" Notebook file and go to page 2. Ask students to think of a fiction book to recommend. Hold partner conversations, allowing each student two minutes to present the case for their book. Afterward, ask students to make notes on their individual whiteboards about:

- what they now know about the other book
- whether they have been persuaded to read it, and the reasons for their decision
- a score out of 10 for the speaker's powers of persuasion

Write or type examples of students' notes in the space provided on the Notebook file.

Mini-Lesson

1. Go to page 3 of the Notebook file. Ask students to work in pairs to think of questions they would ask before choosing a book as their reading book. Ask them to write their top three questions on their individual whiteboards.
2. Share results, annotating the Notebook file by writing numbered questions in the boxes on page 3.
3. Randomly, give partners a chapter book. Each book must have a summary book blurb (probably on the back cover). Ask students to read only the blurb. Invite them to check the questions on the Notebook page and note, on their whiteboards, the numbers answered.
4. Share results. Write an answer, when supplied, in a different color under the questions on page 3.
5. Investigate the blurb formed by these answers. Ask questions such as: *What sort of picture is built up by this imaginary book? What picture would suit the cover? Did your blurb give additional information?* Discuss the points raised.
6. Move on to page 4. Explain the context: a book review in a magazine for teachers. The review should help a teacher identify if the book will suit a class. Read and discuss the review, emphasizing that while there is enough information to promote interest in the book, there is not so much of the story that there is no point in reading the book.
7. Investigate the text, applying questions from page 3. Point out if and where they are answered.

Independent Work

Display page 5 of the Notebook file. Present the following scenario: You want to compile a resource for next year's class. It will be a collection of reviews to help students choose a book. Ask students to write a book review for your collection. Suggest that they review a book they have read this year. Encourage them to start by writing a brief synopsis of the book to remind themselves of the content.

Wrap-Up

Invite students to write or type their reviews on page 6 of the Notebook file. Point out how writers of book reviews offer tempting details without revealing the whole plot.

Verbs and Tenses

Learning objectives
- To understand verb tenses—past, present, and future.
- To know and apply common spelling rules for verb endings.

Resources
- "Verbs and Tenses" Notebook file
- paper and pens

Whiteboard tools
- Pen tray
- Highlighter pen
- Select tool
- On-screen Keyboard

Getting Started

Review the term *verb*. Define a verb as a doing or being word. It can express an action, a happening, a process, or a state. Remind students that:

- every sentence needs a verb;
- a verb can be a chain of words.

Open the Notebook file "Verbs and Tenses" and look at the text on page 2. Together, read the passage, identify the verbs, and highlight them.

Mini-Lesson

1. Go to page 3 of the Notebook file. The three hyperlinked soccer buttons lead to the invitation to Max's party, the voiceover Max wrote to go with a video of the day, and the entry Max wrote in his diary at the end of the day.
2. Press the soccer ball next to "The invitation." Read it and together identify the verbs. Ask volunteers to highlight them. Reveal correct answers by pressing the button.
3. Move to Max's voiceover. Press on the text to hear Max's voiceover. Repeat the process, highlighting the verbs first, and then checking the answers.
4. For Max's diary, ask students to drag the verbs into the text before pressing the button to check that they are correct.
5. Challenge students to explain the difference between the verbs in each passage. (They are in different tenses.)
6. Review the word *tense*: The tense of a verb gives information about when the action took place. Identify the tenses of these three pages of information: present, past, and future.
7. Investigate how the tenses are formed. Focus on the verb endings in each text. Point out the frequent use of *-s*, *-ing*, and *-ed*. Explain that these are some of the regular verb endings. If required, use page 7 to write notes about verb tenses and the different verb endings.
8. Look again at the paragraph on page 2. Encourage students to say what tense has been used here. (The present tense)

Independent Work

Ask students to write two more paragraphs on a sheet of paper to continue the text on page 2 of the Notebook file. One paragraph should be about education in the past, the other about education in the future. Students should use the verbs that they highlighted on page 2, but change their tense. Supply opening words for both paragraphs:

- When our great-grandparents were students . . .
- In the future . . .

Wrap-Up

Invite students to share their work. Write examples of their sentences on page 8 of the Notebook file. Discuss the verb forms used. Look for examples of the usual spelling patterns: *-s*, *-ed*, and *-ing*. Identify instances of verbs doubling a consonant (for example, *chats* becomes *chatted*).

Adverbs

Learning objective

- To identify adverbs and understand their function in sentences.

Resources

- "Adverbs" Notebook file
- "The Meeting" (p. 74)

Whiteboard tools

- Pen tray
- Select tool
- Highlighter pen

Getting Started

Look at page 2 of the "Adverbs" Notebook file. Remind students that words belong to different parts of speech. A word's part of speech depends on its function in a sentence. Review familiar parts of speech: verbs and nouns. Ask students to highlight the nouns (*Margaret, labels*) and verbs (*held, looked*). Ask: *What part of speech do the words in red belong to?* Identify them as adverbs. Make a separate list of the adverbs by double-clicking on the text, then highlight each adverb and drag it out of the text box onto the page.

Mini-Lesson

1. Display page 3 of the Notebook file. Explain that an adverb's usual function is to add meaning to a verb.
2. Investigate the adverbs used in the Getting Started text. Point out that most answer the question *How?* (for example, *clearly* explains how the names were written; *shyly* explains how Margaret looked.) Ask students which other adverbs answer the question *How?* (*wearily, tightly,* and *silently*)
3. Focus on the word *Eventually*. Agree that it answers the question *When?*
4. Ask if students have noticed anything special about the spellings of adverbs. Explain that adverbs commonly (but not always) end in *-ly*.
5. Investigate the position of the adverbs. Ask: *Which word does the adverb add meaning to?* (The verb) *Which word should it stay near?* (The verb) *Eventually* is an exception in this text.
6. Suggest improving the text on page 4 with eight to ten adverbs. Share ideas and make additions to the SMART Board. Page 5 demonstrates adverbs that could be used in the text. Warn against unnecessary adverbs, for example, when the verb already expresses the meaning of a suggested adverb.
7. Explain that adverbs are also useful in dialogue passages because they help the reader "see" a speaker's face and "hear" the tone of voice (for example: *"I don't know," John replied glumly*).
8. Encourage students to suggest more adverbs that could describe how people speak, and write a few of their ideas on page 6 (for example: *loudly, quietly, cheerfully, miserably, happily*).

Independent Work

Ask students to complete the dialogue on "The Meeting" (p. 74). Explain that each of the speaking verbs needs an adverb to bring the text to life. The spoken words must suit the adverbs chosen. Provide less-confident learners with a list of adverbs to use.

Wrap-Up

Invite students to share their finished texts. Add examples of their sentences to page 6 of the Notebook file, highlighting the adverbs used. Discuss whether the spoken words suit the adverbs chosen. Let students speak the words in the appropriate voice.

Adjectives

Learning objective

- To show imagination through the language used to create emphasis, humor, atmosphere, or suspense.

Resources

- "Adjectives" Notebook file
- writing notebooks and pens

Whiteboard tools

- Pen tray
- Highlighter pen
- Screen Shade
- Select tool

Getting Started

Open page 2 of the "Adjectives" Notebook file and read the text to students. Question them about their reactions. Ask: *How does the description make you feel? What mood do the words create?*

Now lower the Screen Shade to reveal the second paragraph. Read it to students and repeat the questions. Compare the texts. Ask: *Does the second version make you feel differently when it is read? How? Why?* Note down some comments on the SMART Board. Express the view that the second text arouses expectations, making you want to see what will happen.

Mini-Lesson

1. Highlight the additional words and the changed final word in the second excerpt on page 2 of the Notebook file. Ask students what part of speech these words belong to. (Adjectives)
2. Define *adjective*—a word describing somebody or something. Investigate which nouns are described by the adjectives. Discuss the benefits of adding adjectives to this text. (Tension is built.)
3. Play a game in which students suggest an adjective to describe a given classroom object. Encourage informative or expressive adjectives, rather than bland ones, for example: a *grazed* knee; a *tanned* face; a *modern* computer; a *useless* box.
4. Display page 3 of the Notebook file, read it to students, and discuss it together. How does it make students feel?
5. Point out the word *afraid*. Does this piece of writing make students feel afraid? Suggest that well-chosen adjectives could add to the mood.
6. Work together, experimenting with adding adjectives. Encourage adjectives of sufficient intensity, avoiding those that are too obvious. (An amended version of the text, showing possible adjectives, appears on page 4.)
7. Ask students to think up an imaginary world. List some of their ideas on page 5 of the Notebook file. Some examples are given below, but encourage students' own ideas:
   - A world on the other side of an ordinary doorway
   - A place reached through a theme park ride
   - A house that changes as night falls

Independent Work

Ask students to write a description of their world. They should use well-chosen adjectives to create atmosphere and tension. Suggest writing a rough draft, before editing and producing a polished version (computers would be useful).

Wrap-Up

Invite some students to read their descriptions to the class. Ask listeners to pick out memorable adjectives and list them on page 5 of the Notebook file. Discuss students' reactions to those words.

Parts of Speech, Part 1

Learning objectives
- To identify various parts of speech.
- To know and apply common spelling rules, particularly word endings.

Resources
- "Parts of Speech, Part 1" Notebook file
- "Same Word—Different Endings" (p. 75)

Whiteboard tools
- Eraser
- Pen tray
- Screen Shade
- Highlighter pen

Getting Started

Open page 2 of the "Parts of Speech, Part 1" Notebook file. Discuss the parts of speech with students: *noun, verb, adjective,* and *adverb*. Then use the Eraser from the Pen tray to erase the red marks to reveal the definitions.

Move the Screen Shade to reveal the last sentence on the page. Ask: *Which words are the nouns?* (*teachers; classes*) *Which word is the verb?* (*talked*) Invite students to add an adjective, such as *patient* or *quiet*, and an adverb, such as *loudly* to the sentence. They should then highlight the different parts of speech, using the same colors that are used in the definitions.

Mini-Lesson

1. Go to page 3 of the Notebook file. Point out the words *dined* and *served* and ask: *What do they have in common?* (Both are verbs and end in *-ed*.)
2. Extract *dined* and *served* from the text by double-clicking on the text, highlighting the word, and dragging it out from the text. Invite a student to drag the words into the correct column of the "Parts of Speech" table.
3. Explain that endings can give clues about parts of speech. Elicit the typical ending of a verb. (*-ed*) Put *-ed* under the heading Verb. Identify endings typical of the other parts of speech. Label the headings:
   - Noun (plurals end in): *-s, -es*
   - Adjective: *-er, -est*
   - Verb: *-s, -es, -ed, -ing*
   - Adverb: *-ly*

   Point out endings that are typical of more than one part of speech.
4. Investigate further by finding words to agree with the headings, taking them from the text and moving them into the correct columns.
5. Emphasize that links between word endings and parts of speech are only generalizations and there are many exceptions (for example, *waiter* ends in *-er* but it is not an adjective). Ask: *What part of speech is it?* (A noun)
6. Display page 4. Draw attention to the fact that the two sentences use the same root word repeatedly but in different forms, with different endings, and in different parts of speech.
7. Drag the highlighted words into the correct column on the table. Point out that *actor* and *buzzer* are nouns.
8. Make up more sentences like these. Say the sentences out loud and invite students to write the words in the chart.

Independent Work

Give out copies of "Same Word—Different Endings" (p. 75) and ask students to complete the poem. Emphasize that it does not have to make much sense!

Wrap-Up

Talk about the varied forms of some words used in students' poems, making notes on page 5 of the Notebook file. Invite some of the students to read their poems aloud.

Parts of Speech, Part 2

Learning objective
- To review the different kinds of nouns; the function of pronouns and adverbs; and the agreement between nouns, pronouns, and verbs.

Resources
- "Parts of Speech, Part 2" Notebook file
- "School Life" (p. 76)
- individual whiteboards and pens

Whiteboard tools
- Pen tray
- Select tool
- Text tool
- Highlighter pen

Getting Started

Read the text on page 2 of the "Parts of Speech, Part 2" Notebook file. Test students' knowledge of parts of speech by identifying the part of speech of the highlighted words. Change the color of words to show the different parts of speech.

Review the meanings of the following terms: *nouns*, *pronouns*, *verbs*, and *adverbs*. Pressing on the red box at the bottom of the page brings up the parts of speech and definitions. Point out that the position of adverbs in sentences may vary.

Ask: *Which noun is replaced by* It? (box) Emphasize verb agreement: *was* agrees with *box*; *were* agrees with *dangers*. Experiment with moving *desperately* to a new sentence position for a changed sentence structure. Ask students to identify other examples of these parts of speech.

Mini-Lesson

1. Highlight the nouns on page 2 of the Notebook file. List the different kinds of nouns: singular, plural, collective, proper, noun phrases, noun clauses.
2. Go to page 3 to learn more about these types of nouns.
3. Read the text on page 4. Talk about the highlighted words. Ask which noun group they belong to. (Noun phrases) Identify the main noun in each noun phrase and discuss how it is modified.
4. Drag out the noun phrases and place them in the appropriate columns in the table. Do this by double-clicking on the text, dragging to highlight the word, and dragging it out from the text.
5. Read the text on page 5. Explain that adverbs are hidden in the spaces. In pairs, ask students to write a suggestion for each adverb on their individual whiteboards.
6. After they have done this, pull the screen across the text to reveal the hidden words.
7. Emphasize that alternatives may present a different picture. Write good examples on the Notebook page.

Independent Work

Give out copies of "School Life" (p. 76) and ask students to write a poem about school life. The poem should visit different rooms and places and create images of what is happening there. Discuss some places, characters, and activities to include. Encourage initial rough drafts before writing the poem in neat handwriting. Encourage use of strong verbs, different kinds of nouns, and appropriate adjectives and adverbs. Students should try to follow the pattern set up in the first two lines.

Less-confident learners could work in pairs, speaking lines before writing. As an extra challenge, ask more-confident learners to investigate a paragraph of a novel and identify different kinds of nouns.

Wrap-Up

Ask students to read their "School Life" poems aloud. Small-group work would allow students to use different voices within one poem.

Prepositions

Learning objective
- To identify and classify a range of prepositions.

Resources
- "Prepositions" Notebook file
- "The Second Half" (p. 77)
- individual whiteboards and pens

Whiteboard tools
- Eraser
- Pen tray
- Highlighter pen
- Select tool
- Creative pen

Getting Started

Go to page 2 of the "Prepositions" Notebook file. Explain that Darren has lost his cell phone. Ask students to jot down five phrases (not sentences) on their individual whiteboards of where it could be. Compare answers, and use the Creative pen to mark five suggested places with a star. Beside each star, write an appropriate phrase given by students (for example, *behind the car*; *in the mailbox*; *under his foot*). Select phrases that begin with different prepositions. Press on the car's rear bumper to reveal that the phone is behind the car and in front of the lamp post. Go to page 3 of the Notebook file and repeat the exercise, this time guessing the location of items in the classroom (for example, your glasses). Make notes on the Notebook page.

Mini-Lesson

1. Investigate the phrases on page 2 of the Notebook file. Highlight the prepositions and ask: *What part of speech are they?*
2. Explain that a preposition is usually followed by a noun phrase (for example, *his pocket*). Ask: *What are all these prepositions about?* (They indicate position.)
3. Go to page 4 of the Notebook file. Allow students time to think or discuss with a partner before taking suggestions for prepositions. Annotate each blank with a possible preposition.
4. Ask someone to read the story using a preposition in each blank. Let someone else read a different version, making different selections. (Use the Eraser from the Pen tray to clear the page to add different prepositions.) Point out how different prepositions affect meaning (for example, *before sunrise* or *after sunrise*).
5. Use the Eraser to clear the page and pull the tab across the screen to reveal the author's choices.
6. Highlight *after sunrise*. Ask: *Does* after *indicate position?* (No, it indicates time.)
7. Go to page 5. Explain that prepositions may indicate position, time, direction, possession, instrument, purpose, or accompaniment. Use a Highlighter pen to color-code each type.
8. Investigate and highlight the author's choices in the story on page 4: *What is indicated by each preposition?* Color-code them appropriately.

Independent Work

Give out copies of "The Second Half" (p. 77) for students to complete. They should use between 10 and 15 prepositions with noun phrases. Display page 5 of the Notebook file to remind students of the different uses of prepositions.

Give less-confident learners a list of prepositions to use. Encourage more-confident learners to investigate the prepositions on a page of their current reading book.

Wrap-Up

Select one of the students' story endings and discuss it. Ask the writer to explain what is indicated by the prepositions they used. Does the class agree? Go to page 6 of the Notebook file, and enter prepositions next to the correct headings. Repeat this with some other story endings. Use the voting question on page 7 to discuss the differences between prepositions for direction, purpose, and position.

Word Order

Learning objectives
- To clarify meaning and point of view by using varied sentence structure (phrases, clauses, and adverbials).
- To use commas to mark clauses.

Resources
- "Word Order" Notebook file
- "Changing Order, Changing Meaning" (p. 78)

Whiteboard tools
- Pen tray
- Highlighter pen
- Select tool

Getting Started
Go to page 2 of the "Word Order" Notebook file. Ask students to investigate the sentence pairs. What do they notice? Conclude that the pairs of sentences use the same words but change the word order. Do students think this affects meaning?

Mini-Lesson
1. Investigate the sentences from the Getting Started activity more closely. Discuss sentence types. Explain that:
   - Sentence 1 is a simple sentence (one clause) with an adverb.
   - Sentence 2 is a simple sentence with a prepositional phrase.
   - Sentence 3 is a compound sentence (two equal clauses).
   - Sentence 4 is a complex sentence (one main clause and a subordinate clause).
2. Highlight the words that move in each pair. Identify them:
   - In sentence 1, an adverb is moved.
   - In sentence 2, a prepositional phrase is moved.
   - In sentence 3, the clauses are reversed.
   - In sentence 4, the clauses are reversed.
3. Explain that the type of phrases in these sentences means that the word order can be changed without changing the meaning of the sentence. Point out the punctuation changes that occur: When adverbs and prepositional phrases lead the sentence, a comma follows them in sentences 1 and 2, and a comma separates the main and subordinate clauses in sentence 4.
4. Display page 3 of the Notebook file. Point out that these sentences also use identical words, but their order is changed. Ask: *What else has changed?* (The meaning) Explain that a phrase such as *biggest man* must stay together. If separated, the adjective may describe the wrong noun.
5. Go to page 4 of the Notebook file. Experiment with ordering the words in different ways, typing up different sentences, for example:
   - *The dog bit the man nastily.*
   - *Nastily, the dog bit the man.*
6. Point out punctuation changes for each version.

Independent Work
Ask students to complete "Changing Order, Changing Meaning" (p. 78). Remind them to think about punctuation.

Wrap-Up
Invite students to write their sentences on page 5 of the Notebook file. Look at the sentences, discussing meaning and punctuation. Use students' pictures from the reproducible sheet to show how the meaning of a sentence can change if the word order is changed. Press the red box at the bottom of page 5 of the Notebook file to see the sentences written out in the correct order.

Passive & Active Voices

Learning objective

- To express subtle distinctions of meaning by constructing sentences in varied ways.

Resources

- "Passive & Active Voices" Notebook file
- individual whiteboards and pens

Whiteboard tools

- Pen tray
- Select tool
- Delete button
- On-screen Keyboard

Getting Started

Display page 2 of the "Passive & Active Voices" Notebook file. Review what a *verb* is, then reveal the definition beneath the blue panel. Ask students to write a sentence containing a verb. Write a selection of these in the space provided on the Notebook file.

Use page 3 to review the terms *active* and *passive*. Encourage students to suggest what the terms mean and write their ideas on the Notebook file. Explain that they are the two verb voices. Look at the sentence at the bottom of the page: "The picture was painted by Monet." Ask students: *Is the sentence active or passive?* Press the word *active* or *passive* for sound effects that indicate whether or not they are correct.

Mini-Lesson

1. Go to page 4 of the Notebook file. Explain that most sentences are in the active voice. Discuss the sentence: "The lady bought the car." Check that students recognize the verb (*bought*); the subject of the verb (*lady*); and the object of the verb (*car*). Delete the orange panels to reveal the answers.
2. Explain that sentences in the active voice always follow this pattern: subject–verb–object. Drag the labels to annotate the sentence.
3. Go to page 5. Invite students to write a new active sentence about the lady. Ask students to hold up their boards for you to make a quick check. Tell them to leave the sentences on their individual whiteboards, and add some of their examples to the Notebook file.
4. Display page 6. Explain that in the passive voice, the sentence is turned around, with the subject and object changing places: the subject of the verb becomes the object, for example: "The car was bought by the lady."
5. Draw attention to the pattern for a passive sentence: object–verb–subject. Move the labels to annotate the sentence.
6. Challenge students to write the passive version of the active sentences on their individual whiteboards. Point out where changes in verb forms were needed. Add some examples to page 7.
7. Play the miming game on page 8 together. Write or type some examples of active and passive sentences on the page.
8. Extend the activity on page 9. Encourage students to write an active and a passive sentence on their whiteboards to describe their actions. Add some examples to the corresponding boxes on the Notebook file.

Independent Work

Move on to page 10 of the Notebook file. Ask students to write a newspaper report on events involving the characters in the pictures. Most sentences will be in the active voice, but there must be at least five in the passive voice.

Wrap-Up

Annotate pages 11 to 13 of the Notebook file with some of students' sentences. Ensure that students recognize the subject, verb, and object in the sentences.

Apostrophes & Possession

Learning objective
- To use the apostrophe for possession.

Resources
- "Apostrophes & Possession" Notebook file
- "Animal Possessions" (p. 79)
- individual whiteboards and pens

Whiteboard tools
- Pen tray
- Select tool
- On-screen Keyboard
- Highlighter pen

Getting Started

Display the text on page 2 of the "Apostrophes & Possession" Notebook file. Ask students to read through the first paragraph and look for words that have been "pushed together" (made into contractions). Highlight the contractions in the paragraph. Ask: *What letters have been left out? How should we mark those letters?* (With an apostrophe) Invite volunteers to add the apostrophes and leave the text on the screen.

Mini-Lesson

1. Introduce the term *omission*—letters left out of a shortened form as words are pushed together. Explain that this occurs frequently in speech.
2. Explain that all the apostrophes used in the Getting Started activity are apostrophes of omission. Write an apostrophe in the key at the bottom of the screen, and highlight it with the same color you used before. Beside the apostrophe put *O* for *Omission*.
3. Ask students to read the second paragraph to a partner. Can any of them hear something strange about the words? Compare ideas. Agree that *of* phrases sound clumsy. Ask students what the more usual, economical way is of explaining who owns something. (An apostrophe followed by *s*) Explain that possession is the second use of an apostrophe.
4. Invite students to edit the text to make the changes, highlighting the apostrophes in a second color: *Jasmine's coat was on the floor. Jade's bag was open. The boys' instruction books were torn in half. Students' diaries were open.*
5. Add another apostrophe to the key and highlight it in the second color. Label it *P* for *Possession*.
6. Now go to page 3 of the Notebook file and read out each phrase. Ask students to say the economical, contracted form. Type up the phrases and add a couple more examples of your own.
7. Explain the rules:
   a. Singular owners and other owners not ending in *s*, add *'s*.
   b. Plural owner ending in *s*, just add *'*.

Independent Work

Ask students to complete the "Animal Possessions" poem (p. 79).

Wrap-Up

Use the scanner to upload and view a selection of students' poems on page 4 of the Notebook file. (Add scanned images by selecting Insert, then Picture File, and browsing to where you have saved the image.) Invite poets to read their poems aloud to the rest of the class.

Its and *It's*

Learning objectives

- To use the apostrophe for possession.
- To find out the differences between *its* and *it's*.

Resources

- "Its and It's" Notebook file
- copy of page 7 of the Notebook file for each student

Whiteboard tools

- Eraser
- Pen tray
- Highlighter pen
- Select tool

Getting Started

Play an oral game, asking students simple questions. Encourage informal answers, but in sentences. Use questions containing *is it* or *is* + a singular noun, for example: *What day is it? What time is it? What on earth is wrong with this picture? Whose pen is this?* Extend the game to students asking you questions. Make a point (without mentioning it) of using *it's* instead of *it is* in the answers. Invite students to write a sentence to answer the questions on page 2 of the Notebook file.

Mini-Lesson

1. Display page 3 of the Notebook file. Can students spot a difference between the language of each question and its answer? Listen to students' ideas. Guide them to notice that every question word is written in full. Ask: *Is this true of the answer?* (No)
2. Point out the highlighted *it's* in the two answers. Ask students to name the punctuation mark that has been used here. (An apostrophe) Establish the reason for its use. (To show that a letter has been omitted)
3. Review this use of apostrophes. Explain that we often run words together in speech; in informal writing we can do the same. An apostrophe marks the letter(s) left out.
4. Look at the page again and ask: *Which letter is missing in* it's? (i) *What would be the full form?* (it is)
5. Point out the highlighted *its* in the two sentences on page 4. Ask: *Is an apostrophe needed here?* Guide students to recognize that no letter is missing. Discuss the meaning of *its* here. Agree on the answer "belonging to it."
6. Go to page 5. The sentences from pages 3 and 4 have been repeated for comparison. Ensure that students understand why *its* or *it's* has been used in each case.
7. Display page 6. Ask students to decide and then drag the correct word (*its* or *it's*) to complete the sentences.
8. Challenge students to provide sentences using *its* and *it's* and write them on the board. Highlight the *its* and *it's*.

Independent Work

Display page 7 of the Notebook file and give a printout of the page to each child. Ask students to fill the spaces on their sheets with either *it's* or *its*. Emphasize thinking about what the word means in each sentence.

Encourage less-confident learners to focus on part of the text at a time, advising them of how many of each form to look for. As an extra challenge, ask more-confident learners to add more text with *it's* or *its* sentences.

Wrap-Up

Review the independent work using page 7 of the Notebook file. Use the Eraser from the Pen tray to rub over the spaces on the screen to reveal the correct answers. Ask students to compare the answers on their worksheets with the version on screen. Discuss any misconceptions they may have had.

Punctuation

Learning objectives

- To clarify meaning and point of view by using varied sentence structure.
- To identify the common punctuation marks.

Resources

- "Punctuation" Notebook file
- printouts of pages 6 and 7 for each student
- individual whiteboards and pens

Whiteboard tools

- Pen tray
- Screen Shade
- Highlighter pen
- Select tool

Getting Started

Read the following text aloud. Make sure that punctuation is clear in the way that you read, but do not supply it. Ask students to record on individual whiteboards the number of sentences they hear:

Titus was a Roman, but he was living in Britain. As a centurion, he had charge of 100 men. Although he tried to treat his men well, he knew they missed home. The north of England was unwelcoming. The landscape was bleak; the terrain was difficult. The thing his men hated most was the weather. It was cold and rainy.

Compare answers. Record their answers on page 2 of the "Punctuation" Notebook file.

Mini-Lesson

1. Display the paragraph on page 3 of the Notebook file. Ask students to punctuate it by pressing the punctuation marks and capital letters at the bottom of the page and dragging and dropping them in the appropriate position in the text. Then move the Screen Shade to reveal the correct punctuation.
2. Review the function of capital letters, periods, and commas. Point out that writers' use of commas is very variable; some writers would leave out some of these commas.
3. Go to page 4. Explain that it is possible to link two sentences with colons and semicolons.
4. Explain the use of a colon: to introduce further information. Ask students to show you a place where a colon could be used in the first sentence. *(The thing his men hated most was the weather: it was cold and rainy.)* Invite a volunteer to drag the colon into position and move the Screen Shade to see whether he or she is correct. Explain that the colon emphasizes the link between two statements, the second one now beginning with a small letter.
5. Point out the semicolon. Explain that it can replace a period to link two sentences that are related in meaning and are equally balanced. Ask students where they could use a semicolon in this paragraph. *(The landscape was bleak; the terrain was difficult.)* Again demonstrate, moving the Screen Shade to check. Tell students that semicolons can also be used to separate items in a list.
6. Use the text on page 5 to review the rules for quotation marks: where they are placed, how spoken and unspoken words are separated, and how new paragraphs are used for each speaker. Invite volunteers to add the punctuation. Move the Screen Shade to show the correct punctuation.

Independent Work

Give each child a copy of pages 6 and 7 of the Notebook file. Ask them to add the missing punctuation marks to their sheets. Encourage them to read the sentences aloud to themselves.

Wrap-Up

Invite volunteers to edit the text on screen to add the punctuation on pages 6 and 7 of the Notebook file. After they have done this, delete the box at the foot of each page to check that they are correct.

Name ______________________ Date ____________

A Strange Shopping List

Wilf is a sorcerer's apprentice. The sorcerer asks him to write a shopping list for a spell—but Wilf does it all wrong! The sorcerer needs more than one of everything. Help Wilf by writing a new shopping list.

One spellbook shelf	Five spellbook shelves
One loaf of magibread	______________
One cat's life	______________
One spare shirt cuff	______________
One starry scarf	______________
One dragon knife	______________
One falling leaf	______________
One wooden staff	______________
One green elf	______________
One dandelion puff	______________
One Indian chief	______________
One golden calf	______________

Write the spell that the sorcerer is going to make.

____

____

____

Name ______________________________ Date ______________

Common Endings Crossword

ACROSS

4. The scary spider gave Miss Muffet a ___________.

5. I don't walk under ladders because I am ___________.

8. Another word for *branch* is ___________.

9. The man in the badge and uniform looks ___________.

10. "Two plus two" is an ___________ problem.

11. Harry had a sore throat and a tickly ___________.

12. Our cat is very ___________ and always wants to know what's going on.

13. After the day comes the ___________.

DOWN

1. Pigs eat their food from a ___________.

2. This is a ___________ day for me because it's my birthday.

3. She walked ___________ the open door.

6. Ella didn't go to school in case her illness was ___________.

7. "Five take away three" is a ___________ problem.

Name ______________________ Date __________

Irresistible Crossword

All the answers use prefixes that mean "not" (*ir-, il-, im-, in-*).

ACROSS

4. Has no sense of responsibility

6. Do not give this answer a checkmark

7. Not according to the law

8. Not the proper way to act

9. Not very likely

DOWN

1. Cannot be read

2. At no fixed time

3. Does not like to be active

5. Not able to read or write

6. Cannot be done

1 2 3 4 5 6 7 8 9

Name ______________________________ Date ______________

Word Webs

Complete these word webs.

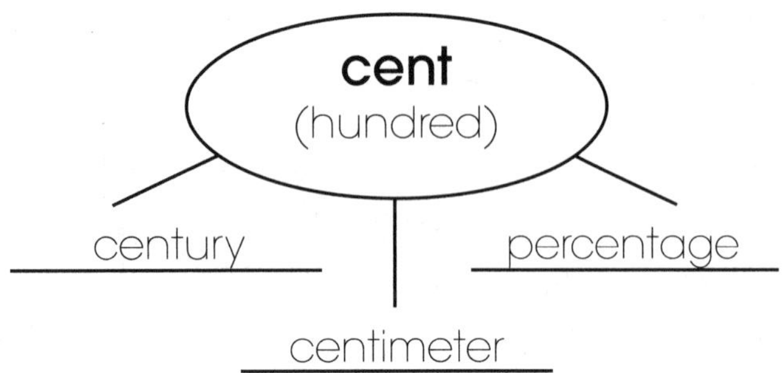

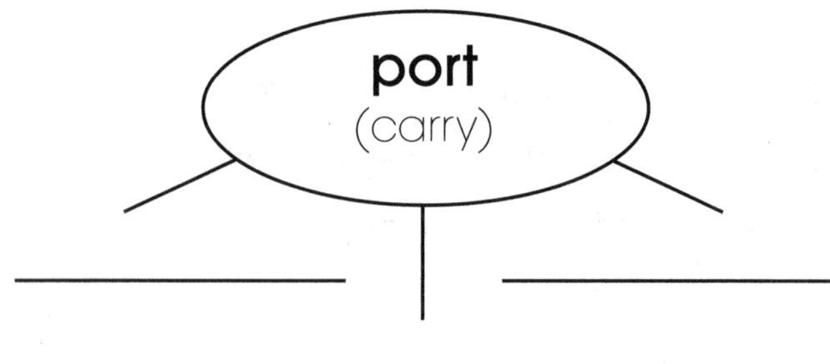

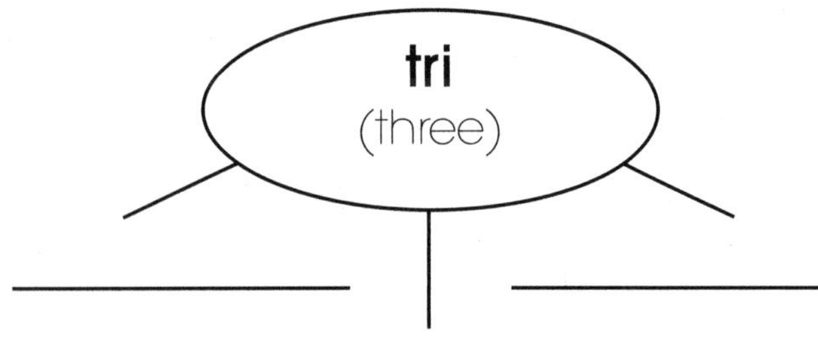

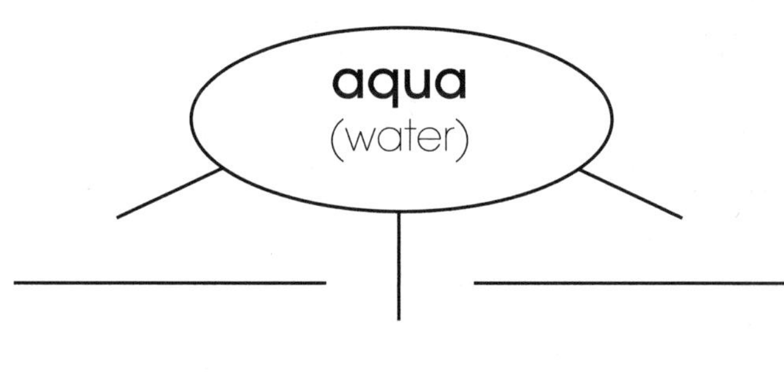

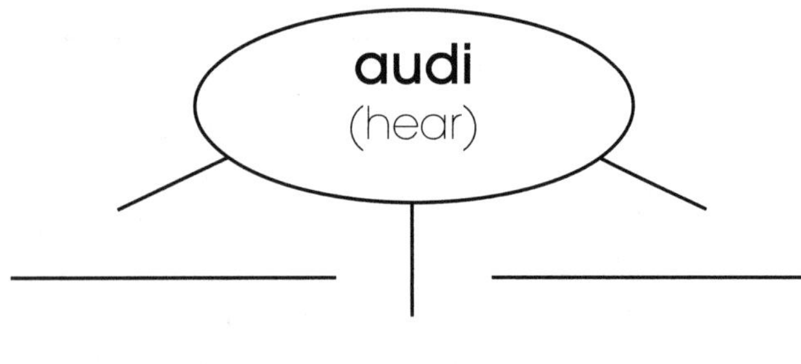

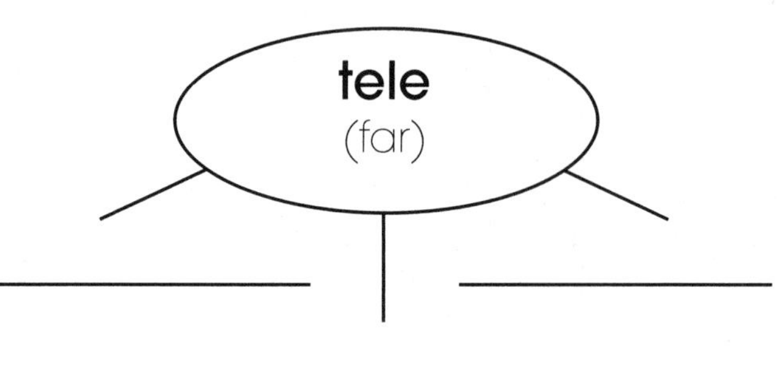

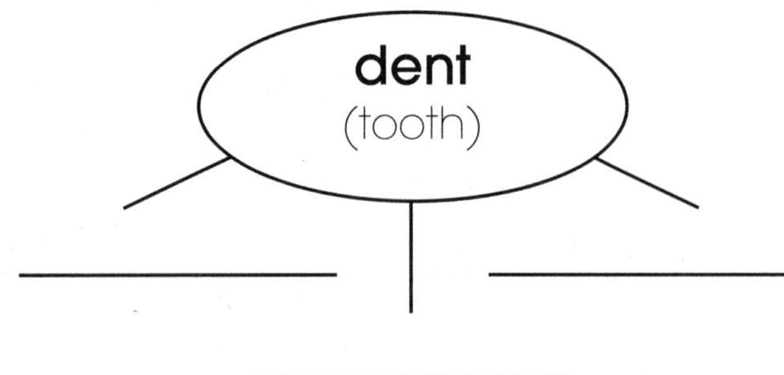

fort
(strong)

Name ______________________________ Date ______________

Word Clusters

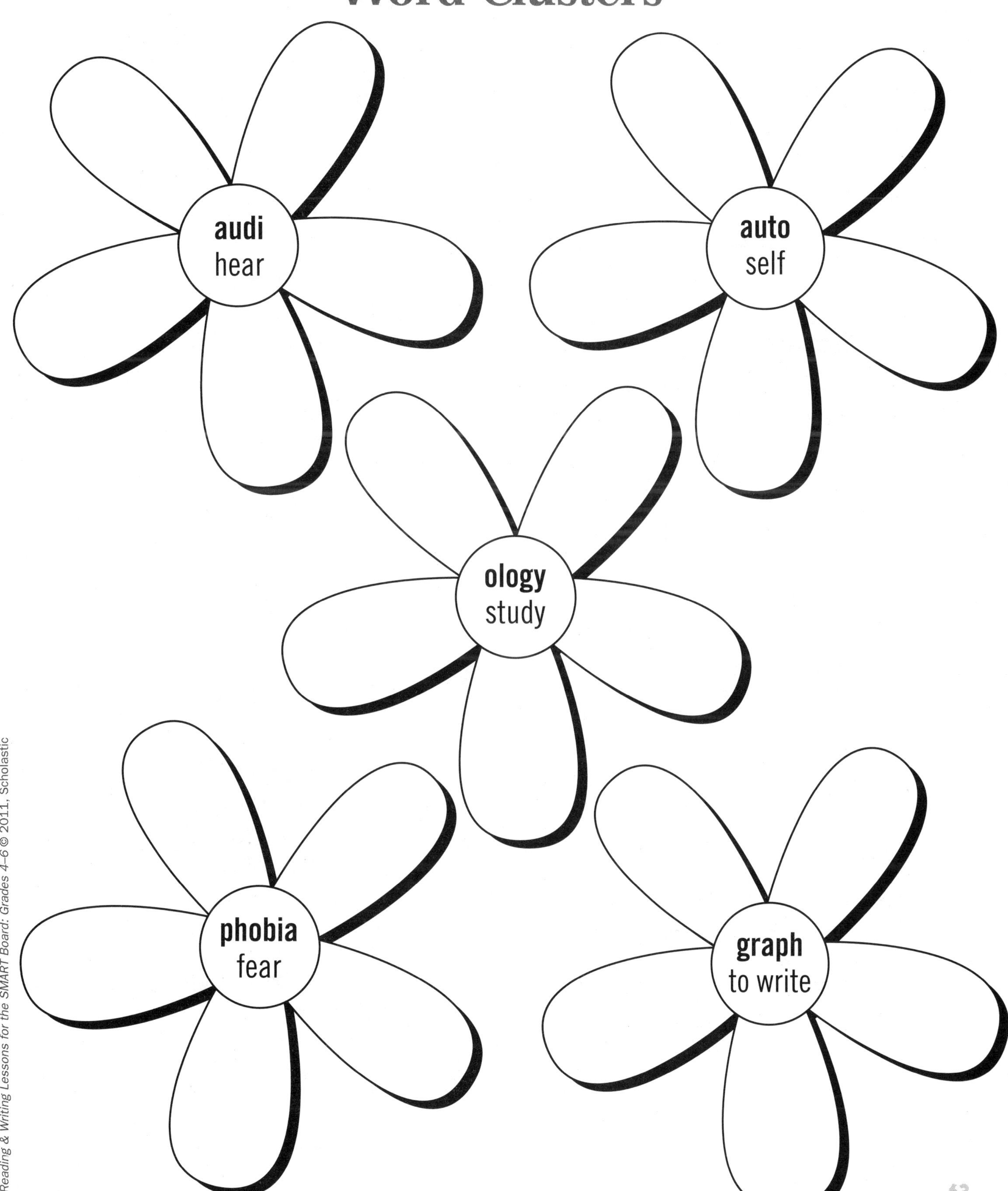

Name ______________________________ Date ______________

Unusual People

My family
My sister is a vaccaphobe,
She won't go in a field.
My Dad has got octophobia
He dreads ________________.

My teachers
One teacher takes ambology,
She's always on the move.
Another does finology;
He hates ________________.

My friends
Bert has bought a novatele,
The latest remote control;
____
________________________.

Myself
I want to be a monoastra,
The only one on stage;
____
________________________.

vacca – cow
porc – pig
astra – star
nova – new
super – above (greater)
photo – light
clude – shut
ambul – walk
geo – earth
tele – far off
graph – to write
hydro/a – water
oct – eight
scope – look
mono – alone
fin – end
port – carry
micro – small
phobia – fear
ology – study
fort – strong
dent – tooth
ped – foot

Name ________________________________ Date ______________

Letter to Mom

Use the words from the Homophones box to complete the letter.

________________ Mother,

________________ can't imagine how cold it is ________________! I have ________________ warm clothes. Tomorrow we march north to Eburacum. From ________________ we go to a ________________ near the dreaded Picts. It will ________________ even colder there, I am told. We ________________ freeze. I am going to help build a wall as high as ________________ men. We will guard it day and ________________: the Roman ________________ will watch everywhere. The enemy will not get ________________ our defense. It will be ________________ difficult!

Only ________________ years to go before I return across the ________________ to Italy. I can't ________________ —what a ________________ celebration there will be when we get back! ________________ to me with the news from home.

Your loving ________________, Titus

HOMOPHONES

their/there/they're	place/plays	deer/dear
to/two/too	mite/might	weight/wait
no/know	for/four	threw/through
eye/I	sun/son	grate/great
bee/be	knight/night	ewe/you/yew
see/sea	right/write	hear/here

Name ______________________ Date ____________

Story Planner

3. Climax

____

____

2. Build-up

____

____

4. Resolution

____

____

1. Introduction

____

____

5. Ending

____

____

Name ______________________________ Date ______________

Mapping Texts

Story title:	
Character names:	
1.	2.
3.	4.
5.	6.
7.	8.
9.	

Name ______________________________ Date ______________

Penguins

Facts:

downy feathers under waterproof feathers; clumsy movements on land; thick layer of fat; fat keeps it warm; graceful swimmer; streamlined shape is good for swimming; is adapted to cold weather; waterproof feathers on outside

Version 1

The penguin has waterproof feathers. It has a thick layer of fat and this fat keeps it warm. It has clumsy movements on land. It has downy feathers under its waterproof feathers. It is adapted to cold weather. It has a streamlined shape. This is good for swimming.

Version 2 (Improve sentence order.)

Version 3 (Add detail, improve structure, and make links.)

Name ________________________________ Date ______________

Paragraph Planning

Plan the next six paragraphs in "Online Progress."

Stage 1: Labels

Stage 2: Details

Stage 3: Opening Words

Name ______________________ Date __________

A Seaside Trip

A seaside trip

is the best of treats because you can
bake hot
cool off
surf waves
slurp drinks
lick lollies
scale rocks
tunnel under
slide dunes
see shells
sail boats
enjoy sun
have fun
at the beach side, seaside.

(by Eileen Jones)

Name ______________________________ Date ______________

Reading Journal Entry

Complete the reading journal entry below.

Date: ______________________________

Title of book: ______________________________

Author: ______________________________

The cover

Where I am up to in the book

My thoughts at the moment

What I think will happen

Name ________________________________ Date ______________

Poem Interpretation

Title ________________________________

Poet ________________________________

Mood of poem

____

____

____

The images I see

____

____

____

Examples of word play

____

____

____

Double meanings

____

____

____

My feelings about the poem

____

____

____

Name ______________________ Date __________

Identify the Text Type

persuasion

instructions

description

explanation

recount

discussion

1. Vitamins

There are about 20 different vitamins. They are usually referred to by a letter of the alphabet. Main ones include:

D – This is found in eggs, butter, and fish. It can also be obtained from sunlight. Vitamin D keeps bones and teeth strong. Lack of this vitamin can lead to weak bones.

C – Vitamin C is present in ...

2. Condensation takes place when a gas is turned into a liquid. It is an essential part of the water cycle. As water vapor formed during evaporation rises into the air, so the vapor is cooled. As a result, condensation occurs and water is released from the clouds. Once it is released, it falls as rain.

3. I promise you that our kitchens are second to none. Our team does a brilliant job. The fitters leave no mess, so you have no cleaning up to do. In order not to inconvenience you, we do everything in one day. In order to help you further, we keep our prices low. Come and check out our showroom so that you can see for yourself.

4.

1. First, mix the fat and sugar together until soft.
2. Next, add the eggs one at a time, beating well.
3. Then, stir in the flour and chocolate powder with a metal spoon.
4. Stop when there is no trace of powder.
5. Pour the mixture into the cake pan.
6. Leave the filled cake pan to stand for three minutes.
7. Finally, cook the mixture in a hot oven until set.

5. My vacation last year was the best ever. I went with a group of friends on a golfing holiday to the Algarve in Portugal. We played golf on a different course every day: first we played Vale de Cobo; then Sole Viste; and finally Villamoure Rio. We repeated the cycle three times. By the end of nine days, I felt like a professional!

6. Obviously, there are valid points on both side of the debate. The children need a new sports field and Harbour Fields is a large site. On the other hand, the asking price is high so the school cannot afford that field and new computers. A sensible way forward is to search for a cheaper site, so that the school can have new computers and a new sports field.

Name ______________________________ Date ______________

The Meeting

There was a lively meeting of the class council that week. Fourth-grade students were discussing class rules, and they had a lot to say.

"Play time is too short," Matt called ______________________.

"______________________," Miss Bramble replied ______________________.

"______________," he continued ______________________.

"______________________," Rafael muttered ______________________.

Jez spoke ______________: "______________"

"______________________," Miss Bramble answered ______________________.

One girl said ______________, "______________________"

One boy asked ______________, "______________________?"

"______________________," Matt interrupted ______________________.

"______________________," Miss Bramble said ______________________.

Name ______________________________ Date ______________

Same Word—Different Endings

Finish this poem using the same words but with different endings

The player, playing, played in plays.

The sailor sailed in a sailing ship with sails.

The worker ______________________________

______________, skipping, ______________________________

______________, ______________, ______________in some shops.

____

____

____

____

____

____

____

____

Helpful words

play	work	shop	skip	hop	look	teach
farm	sail	look	act	help	fish	write
speak	care					

Helpful word endings

-er -s -es -ing -ed -ly -ful

Name ______________________________ Date ____________

School Life

By the school gates, moms and dads, chatting cheerfully,

In the coatroom, noisy children, hanging coats up,

____

____

____

____

____

____

____

____

____

____

____

____

____

____

____

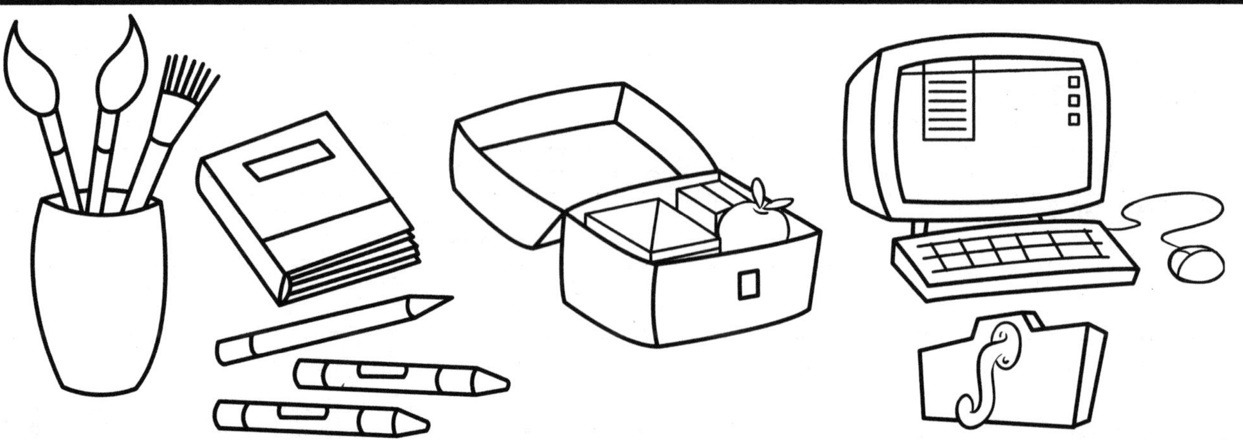

Name ____________________ Date ____________

The Second Half

1. Complete the story. Remember to include prepositions.

2. Highlight each preposition and noun phrase and give it a number. Then decide which column each phrase goes into in the table below, and write in its number.

Position	Time	Direction	Possession	Instrument	Purpose	Accompaniment

Name ______________________ Date ____________

Changing Order, Changing Meaning

Use each row of words to make two different sentences.

1. everyone the remembers Henry VIII name of

a ______________________

b ______________________

2. six Henry had wives divorces and some

a ______________________

b ______________________

3. the king eventually to Pope the spoke selfish

a ______________________

b ______________________

4. Pope order asked Henry the for permission in to the law break special

a ______________________

b ______________________

5. Pope's unfortunately the to request answer was no Henry's

a ______________________

b ______________________

6. Catherine the in Henry end sent away

a ______________________

b ______________________

Draw two pictures to go with one of your pairs of sentences:

Name ______________________________ Date ____________

Animal Possessions

The giraffe's neck is a useful ladder,

The kangaroo's pouch is the baby's cot,

The ______________________________

The ______________________________

The ______________________________

The ______________________________

The ______________________________

The ______________________________

The ______________________________

The ______________________________

The ______________________________

The ______________________________

Notes